To Gu

C000260123

Can God Help M.E?

God Bless

'More than a God spot ... it can be recommended to any sufferers and their relations and friends for its general information about the illness alone ... The second half of the book is a non-pulpit-thumping discussion on spiritual help.'
The Chartered Society of Physiotherapy

'This is the most generally informative and helpful book on ME that I've ever read.'
The Association of Christian Counsellors

'This is an excellent book; I was riveted right from the introduction! It's the best book on ME I've ever read ... a must for anyone interested in ME.'
Jennifer Rees Larcombe

Can God Help M.E?
Bringing Hope to Sufferers of Chronic Fatigue Syndrome

Liz Babbs

Authentic

09 08 07 06 05   7 6 5 4 3 2 1

First published 1999 by Eagle.
This revised and updated edition published 2004 by
Authentic Media, 9 Holdom Avenue, Bletchley, Milton Keynes, Bucks,
MK1 1QR, UK
and PO Box 1047, Waynesboro, GA 30830-2047, USA.

British Library Cataloguing in Publication Data

A catalogue record for this book is available from the
British Library

1-86024-509-9

Cover design by River
Print management by Adare Carwin
Printed in Denmark by Nørhaven Paperback

In memory of my dad,
whose depth of faith in God, despite his
being terminally ill,
challenged me to search for the Truth.

CONTENTS

ACKNOWLEDGEMENTS

Firstly, I'd like to thank my family for their love and support while I've been writing this book. I'd also like to thank David Wavre for initially publishing *Can God Help ME?* in 1999 and Malcolm Down of Authentic Media for his enthusiasm in wanting to republish it. My prayer support group have been wonderful too, and continue to pray faithfully for me and my work. Thanks also to my friends Stella Brookes, Jacquie Anderson, Dr Honor Day and Anthony Green for their artistic contribution, and to Sister Theresa Margaret for letting me use two of her drawings from *Open to God*. Finally, I remain indebted to the many ME sufferers who have become my friends across the years and who have 'walked with me' as I've been writing this book. *Can God Help ME?* is a testimony to their faith and courage in being willing to make themselves vulnerable and to share openly for the benefit of others.

FOREWORD

Are you suffering from that mysterious illness ME? Or are you caring for someone suffering from its debilitating effects? Are you simply wanting to glean more information about the illness? Or do you delight in discovering the treasures that are hidden in the darkness of suffering? Then I have no hesitation in recommending this beautiful book.

In it, the author takes us on a journey. As we travel, as a result of the author's thorough research, our eyes are opened to the nature of ME and the effect it can have on its victims. We also find ourselves surrounded by sufferers from the illness: sufferers who seem full of integrity and longing, many displaying remarkable creativity. And we find ourselves catching the author's genuine compassion for suffering humanity.

Such compassion comes, curiously, without heaviness or despair. Instead, as the journey continues, hope is born as the focus gradually changes and God is brought centre-stage. The author divulges how God can and does break through the gloom and seeming stalemate of the sickness: sometimes, as in her own life, bringing complete and instant healing, sometimes injecting peace into the pain, and always offering the sufferer unconditional love. Treasures in darkness indeed!

I first encountered the author when she was herself grounded by ME. Over the years I have marvelled as I witnessed a quiet miracle: not simply physical healing, but the way God has drawn Liz deeper into a love that has remoulded her, deepened her prayer life and entrusted her with a unique and effective ministry of retreat-giving to ME sufferers. As the book goes to print, I rejoice with Liz and those whose lives have been touched by her infectious enthusiasm and care – and I simply bow before the Mystery of who God is, praying that this quietly joy-filled book may bring hope to many.

Joyce Huggett

INTRODUCTION

I can hardly believe that it is now thirteen years since I had ME. Time has gone by so quickly, yet I'm aware that for many sufferers those thirteen years will have marked only part of an indefinite sentence – an enforced imprisonment, locked inside this illness.

I remember very clearly my own years of incarceration, yet the illness marked a turning point for me. It is interesting that the Oxford Dictionary definition of 'crisis' is 'turning point, especially of disease'. I could never have believed how radically my values would change as the things that previously seemed very important to me were painfully stripped away. I, like many sufferers I talk to, have found new hope and vision despite the illness.

While I was ill, I remember describing ME as 'God's ultimate punishment', and that is what it felt like. I was angry with God and reasoned that this illness was some kind of divine retribution for past misdemeanours. In latter years, I have come to realize that my perception of God was faulty and that it had been conditioned by my upbringing and education.

ME, like many serious illnesses, raises some of the most challenging questions we may ever face. 'What is happening to me?' 'Why me?' 'Why suffering?' 'Is there a God out there?' 'If there is a God, why is he allowing this to happen to me?' 'Can God help me?' Coming to terms with some of these questions can become a transforming part of the journey through this illness. As human beings we are not just mind and body, but spirit too. If we

11

overlook this we deny ourselves the integration and wholeness that has the potential to transform our situation.

ME is an illness that affects so many lives. Virtually everyone I meet seems to know someone with it, whether it be a relative, friend, neighbour, colleague or acquaintance. It is a bewildering illness to suffer from and for others to understand. This book is written both for sufferers and for their friends, families, colleagues, counsellors or pastors, in fact anyone who wants to deepen their understanding of the illness. It is only as we become more aware of the devastating effects of ME that we will be better equipped to reach out to those suffering in our own communities.

In 1991, shortly after I was healed of ME, I sensed God was telling me that I was to write a book and that it would be called *Can God Help ME?* In 1994, I wrote about my own personal journey through ME for a Master's degree. Limited publication and distribution of my dissertation provoked very positive feedback and provided a stepping stone to this book. There are many medical books and autobiographies written on ME, but my aim is to explore the spiritual dimension of having this illness. I hope to take sufferers on a journey where they can discover for themselves an answer to the question, 'Can God help ME/me?'

I'm particularly keen for sufferers to have the opportunity to voice their feelings freely, rather than be represented as a series of case studies, as they are in many books on ME. This book is therefore full of material from the many sufferers I know and have known across the years. I am also indebted to those sufferers who have been on my ME retreats. Their combined wisdom and depth of faith have both challenged and inspired me. As I continue to meet and hear of so many sufferers who have been healed of ME, as well as those whose relationship with God has been totally transformed through this illness, I am convinced that God does have a voice on this subject and that God can help ME.

1

WHAT IS ME?

I'm squeezed out, threatened, uncomfortable. I want to get up and do something. It feels like I've been locked in darkness for ages. It's uncomfortable, threatening, engulfing, suffocating, strangling, destructive. Other people lead busy lives –it's not fair! Fear of the past, and an inability to look forward. I feel chained and trapped. I'm in a time warp –a tunnel without any windows. I feel stifled and choked and I DON'T WANT TO BE HERE!

This is a transcription of the feelings I expressed when I had ME. ME, or myalgic encephalomyelitis (also myalgic encephalopathy), is a physically debilitating illness which is listed as a disease of the nervous system by the World Health Organisation. The Chief Medical Officer's Report issued in January 2002 recognized that 'CFS/ME should be classified as a chronic condition with long-term effects on health'. It is estimated that there are up to 240,000 sufferers in the UK (though this may be a conservative estimate because of the difficulties in diagnosis) and that 25,000 of these sufferers are children, with cases being reported in children as young as three. It has a higher incidence in the population than multiple sclerosis, yet little is known about it.

The illness is characterized by chronic disabling fatigue as well as a variety of other symptoms. It commonly affects healthy, industrious, active people. Many people are affected in the prime of their lives, between 20 and 40, when hopes and aspirations run high. Coping with disablement, curtailment of career prospects and financial uncertainty can become an unbearable strain.

When I developed ME, I was a hyperactive 29-year-old. I taught English and Drama full-time at a comprehensive school as well as on Saturday mornings. I was studying for a Diploma in Special Needs at university and any spare time was filled with sporting activities and socialising. In April 1989, I returned from a skiing trip to Andorra and within a few days developed a flu-like illness which proceeded to tear my life apart. I could hardly recognize myself. What had I become? What was happening to me? Surely I would get better soon. People recover from flu, don't they?

It felt as though somebody had pulled out my plugs. The profound disabling fatigue seemed to strike very suddenly and for no apparent reason. My muscles were severely affected and at times I had to crawl to get to the bathroom. The brain fatigue, or 'fog', as some sufferers call it, is possibly one of the most difficult aspects of the illness to deal with. Coping with a body that won't work is bad enough, but to have a brain that won't function properly is unbearable. When I tried to write, not only could I not spell, but my letters reversed – and to think I was an English teacher!

My visits to the doctor became regrettably frequent. She continued to give me sick notes, not really knowing what was wrong with me, and as time progressed, I realized the depressing fact that I would not be going back to school. The insensitivity of my doctor at that time did not help matters. Like many others, I have had to endure derogatory comments from doctors, friends, family and employers. I felt like saying, 'Would anyone in their right mind choose this lifestyle?' Are all 240,000 sufferers with ME imagining that they are ill? No, certainly not. Just because a disease can't yet be seen under a microscope, does not mean that it does not exist.

Why All the Controversy? What's in a Name?

ME has been a subject of controversy for some time now. No one has yet suggested a name for the illness that everyone agrees with, and so it has undergone several name changes over the years, including Icelandic disease, post-polio syndrome, Epstein Barr virus, Royal Free disease, epidemic neuromyesthenia, yuppie flu, and post-viral fatigue syndrome.

The illness is also now called Chronic Fatigue Syndrome (CFS). But this is a vague and unhelpful name because it is an umbrella term for any condition characterized by chronic fatigue. So the term ME/CFS is now being used more widely. In the US it is referred to as Chronic Fatigue and Immune Dysfunction Syndrome (CFIDS). However, as the illness still tends to be more commonly known and referred to as ME, that is the name I will use in this book.

In 1957 there was an outbreak of ME in London. Some 292 members of the medical, nursing, ancillary and administrative staff of the Royal Free Hospital were affected, but only 12 patients. It was the most physically active people who contracted the illness, which was then named Royal Free disease. Dr Melvin Ramsay, a consultant physician at the hospital, described the organic nature of this illness and suggested it be called myalgic encephalomyelitis. He chose this name because it described the main symptoms: myalgia –

muscle pain, and encephalomyelitis – inflammation of the brain.

In 1970, however, Drs McEvedy and Beard, two psychiatrists with no experience of the disease, re-examined all the case notes. They effectively redefined it by describing the illness at the Royal Free as 'mass hysteria'[1]. This seemed to imply that the illness was 'all in the mind' of sufferers. Dr Melvin Ramsay wrote:

> So radically did McEvedy and Beard influence medical opinion that when I have attempted to put the case for an organic explanation of the disease to younger present-day consultants I have en-countered an attitude of pitying disbelief and the remark, 'Oh, but that was long ago shown to have been as a result of "mass hysteria"'.[2]

The debate over whether the illness is physical or psychological still rages. Doctors remain divided over whether it has a definite organic basis or is simply a form of depression, even though there is now so much evidence outlining its physical origin (see Appendix 1). Unfortunately, years of prejudice have left their mark.

What Causes ME?

Theories vary on this. As Dr Anne Macintyre, an ME sufferer, comments:

> Virologists find ME is usually caused by a virus.
> Immunologists find ME is a disordered immune system.
> Clinical ecologists say ME is a condition of multiple food and chemical allergies.

Psychiatrists decided (many years ago) that ME is a psychiatric illness – i.e. we are mad.

Neurologists think ME is a disorder of the nervous system.[3]

The illness sometimes develops gradually, but acute onset is often triggered by a flu-like infection. Early research suggested a viral origin of this disease, possibly involving an enterovirus. Enteroviruses affect the muscle and nerves, the two main tissues affected by ME. The body's immune system may have been weakened through excessive stress or strain at the time of an infection, becoming unable to make the necessary response. Other research suggests that the immune system may be stimulated into overactivity by an infection, vaccination, exposure to chemicals such as organophosphates, or some other trigger. It is also thought that sufferers may have an inherited pre-disposition to the illness. Some sufferers develop ME following glandular fever. The Epstein Barr virus is thought to cause glandular fever and this is why it was once called chronic Epstein Barr virus. Many symptoms experienced by sufferers of Gulf War Syndrome are also experienced by ME sufferers and so the two have been linked.

But there is progress

It is encouraging to see the progress that is being made in research. Negative attitudes are now being more readily challenged and the general public seems more aware of the illness. There is still some confusion, because the precise cause remains unknown, and a definitive test is not yet available. However, as research continues across the world, it should be possible, in time, to find the cause as well as develop a possible cure.

Who Gets ME?

Anyone of any age can get ME, although it is more common in women, and particularly women between the ages of 20 and 40. It has been described all over the world, principally in developed countries. ME particularly seems to affect those in education and the health services, where there is an increased risk of infection. I have met sufferers from a variety of backgrounds, including teachers, students, dancers, musicians, accountants, doctors, nurses, missionaries, vicars, nuns, monks, an Olympic shot-putter and a clown!

Well-known people with ME

ME may have been around for many centuries. Florence Nightingale is thought to have developed something similar after she caught Crimean fever. The effects of that illness coupled with overwork led her to spend long periods of time resting.

Round the world yachtswoman Clare Francis is founding Patron of the charity Action for ME and has done much to publicize the illness as well as pioneer change.

Lord Puttnam, producer of the film *Chariots of Fire*, suffers with ME and is Patron of Action for ME.

The Duchess of Kent was reported in 1996 to be suffering with ME and had to limit her public engagements. The Duke of Kent is Patron of the charity The ME Association.

The Dean of Westminster, the Very Reverend Michael Mayne, had ME and wrote a book about his experience, *A Year Lost and Found*. He is a former Vice-President of the ME Association.

Esther Rantzen has publicized the plight of ME sufferers, especially young sufferers. Her daughter Emily developed ME after glandular fever. Esther is President of the Association of Youth with ME (AYME) and Vice-President of the National ME Centre.

What Does ME Feel Like?

Sufferers express their views:

- *An utterly miserable existence.*
- *Like living in a dead body.*
- *Awful –I don't know how else to describe it. Just awful.*
- *Being cut off from the river of life.*
- *Like being invisible in an active world that you are no longer a part of.*
- *It confines, constricts, diminishes and confuses. It is a most negative and sterile condition.*
- *At times it consumes me and I feel that I no longer exist as a person but as an illnss.*
- *Like your life has been stolen from you.*
- *It makes me feel a failure as a wife and a mother, as I don't have the energy to offer others.*

I remember describing my illness as a 'goldfish bowl existence'. I was no longer able to participate in life. I had become a spectator staring out from within my own personal prison. Sometimes the walls of that prison seemed to expand, but frequently they seemed to contract, pressing in on me still further. I wrote the following to a penfriend also with ME:

I feel like a 90-year-old inside a 30-year-old body. I hate this enforced imprisonment. I just feel like screaming out at times because you just can't make people understand what it's like. . . . In the end you have to try and find your own kind of peace, which isn't easy.

What happens to the body and mind in ME is frightening. I've listed below some of the main symptoms experienced by sufferers, although I have heard it said that there can be over one hundred different symptoms associated with the illness.

1. Overwhelming and persistent fatigue, usually accompanied by muscle pain, precipitated and aggravated by relatively trivial exercise.
2. Flu-like symptoms, nausea etc.
3. Neurological disturbances: poor memory and concentration, abnormal sleep and temperature regulation, vision and hearing problems, difficulty focusing, tinnitus.
4. Emotional oversensitivity, anxiety, despair and depression.
5. A fluctuating course alternating between relapse and remission.

What are the hardest aspects of the illness to deal with?

I put this question to some of the sufferers I know, and here is what they said:

- *The nausea and sickness, always affecting concentration and enjoyment of activities. The sense of isolation and loneliness.*
- *Losing the whole of my twenties and now, at 31, the possibility of my thirties too.*
- *Joining in activities with my family. I look around the house and see all the things that need doing and I can't do them. That's very depressing.*

- *Not being able to plan ahead, and if I do, often having to cancel at the last minute because I'm not well enough.*
- *Knowing that I'm putting a lot of pressure on my family when they have to do housework, shopping, ironing etc.*
- *The unknown. ME's unpredictability.*
- *The frustration and loss of self-worth.*
- *Looking back I had high hopes that in a few months I'd be better, but as the years go by those hopes diminish.*
- *My career and any chance of promotion.*
- *Family life —school concerts, cricket matches etc. Freedom to be able to plan a weekend away.*
- *People telling you that there is nothing wrong with you. To snap out of it. People putting words into your mouth, saying you are getting well when you are not, and saying you look well when you feel absolutely disgusting!*
- *Losing my mother, who died six weeks ago. She had been caring for me, because my husband, who doesn't believe in ME, left me.*

The prognosis – when will I get better?

This can be variable and unpredictable, because after the initial acute illness, most patients follow a relapsing and remitting course. Clinical observation suggests that 20 per cent of ME sufferers recover within two years, usually those who have been diagnosed early and are able to have sufficient rest. Another 60 per cent learn how to manage their illness through reduced lifestyles, though few can handle a full-time job, and 20 per cent unfortunately gradually deteriorate and become permanently disabled.

2

WHERE CAN I GET HELP AND SUPPORT?

Helping Together

When I wrote my dissertation in 1994, one of the concerns I had expressed was that there seemed to be a real lack of unity between charities, which was not helping the ME cause. So I was delighted to read that in November 1995 the various ME charities had formed an alliance. The ME Alliance now includes the three main charities: the ME Association, Action for ME, and the National ME Centre. Their aim is 'to work together to secure improved recognition, care, support, and information for all those whose lives are affected by ME/CFS'. The addresses of these charities are listed in Appendix 2 at the back of this book.

I was a member of both the **ME Association** and **Action for ME** when I was ill, and found the latest research together with local and national information invaluable. Both these charities have a series of excellent leaflets that can take the hard work out of explaining the illness to employers, doctors, family and friends. Many of these guidelines are also now directly available on the Internet, making it simple for your doctor or employer to access relevant information. Action for ME offers various forms of telephone assistance, including a support and information service, a counselling service and a welfare rights help line. The charity also offers a wide variety of special interest groups and works closely with a series of local support groups across the country. Keeping in touch with other sufferers is important, as it helps to reduce the sense of isolation.

Westcare is another wonderful charity, which has now merged with Action for ME. I met Dr Richard Sykes, the founder and director, in 1990, when I attended Westcare's first respite week. I still have many fond memories of that week and will never forget the care and compassion shown by Richard Sykes and the rest of the Westcare team. During that week I made many long-standing special friendships and, although I didn't realize it at the time, it proved to be a turning point in my management of the illness. (I will be explaining more about the value of respite care and retreats in Chapter 8.) Westcare has a clinic for sufferers and their families in Bristol which offers information, management advice and counselling.

The National ME Centre, founded in the early 1990s, grew out of an increasing need for sufferers to discuss their problems with other sufferers. The Centre introduces sufferers to the techniques of ME treatment and management developed by its Medical Advisor, Dr Leslie Findley, in co-operation with an occupational therapist. Sufferers need to be referred by their doctors. The centre is also linked to the regional neurological unit at Old Church Hospital, Romford, which offers in-patient assessment and rehabilitation.

What if My Doctor Doesn't Understand?

An accident that resulted in a knee injury reminded me of some of the trauma I had gone through with ME. The difficulty of obtaining a diagnosis, the pain and cost, both emotionally and financially. The sense of being lost somewhere in the sea of the medical system, waiting and waiting to see a consultant. The sheer frustration of not knowing what was wrong with me. Surely a knee is straightforward, isn't it? This experience made me realize what an imprecise science medicine is, and yet we expect doctors to have all the answers – well, they are the experts, aren't they?

ME highlights this inadequacy more than most illnesses. The medical profession clearly does not have all the answers, so it is not surprising that ME sufferers become experts, frantically searching for answers for themselves. One sufferer visited a doctor, only to be told, 'There's nothing wrong with you.' The doctor then said, 'Is there something missing in your life?' 'Yes,' she felt like screaming, *'my health! Can't you see? Can't you help?'* Unfortunately doctors, especially GPs, are trained very generally and so do not necessarily know how to diagnose or treat every illness they meet, and they are unlikely to know much about ME unless they have taken a special interest in it. I think sufferers have an important role to play in educating doctors as well as others about ME. When a doctor is openly hostile, however, this may be impossible. Dr Belinda Dawes writes about this from her own experience:

A ruling by your doctors that your problem is psychological is really a sign that they have run out of ideas. Characterising the problem as being in your mind rather than in your body passes the buck to you and says that it is your fault that you are not getting well, not theirs. From our own experience in 'conventional medicine', we know full well just how much pressure a doctor can experience from the endless stream of patients he or she sees, all of whom expect some sort of miraculous scientific cure. Doctors are only human, and it is no longer sensible for the patient to rely totally on the wisdom and paternalism of their GP. You need to be 'consumerist' about your doctors and to participate in deciding what treatment and what approach is most helpful for you.[1]

Changing doctors

Changing doctors was one of the wisest decisions I made when I was ill. My doctor seemed only mildly interested in what was wrong with me and simply said, 'If I had a magic wand, I'd wave it.' Not a particularly helpful statement. When I saw the other partner in the practice, she completely mishandled the situation and sent me with an emergency form to hospital saying, 'I saw someone last week who had lost their voice like you and they turned out to have throat cancer.' Needless to say, this sent me into absolute panic!

I believe that it is really important to have a doctor who is sympathetic to ME and who can work *with* you. Fortunately, changing doctors is a relatively simple process. When I joined the ME Association and the local support group, I had access to a lot of helpful information, including a list of doctors in my area who were sympathetic to ME. Not only did I change my doctor, but I also found out about Dr Sarah Myhill, who specialized in treating ME sufferers on a private basis. My new doctor was very willing to work in conjunction with her as she assessed me and tried various approaches and treatments. This arrangement offered me such hope at a time when everything seemed futile, and although Dr Myhill readily admits that she did not bring about my radical recovery, I will always be grateful to her for offering me such a lifeline.

At last a diagnosis!

Part of the tension of having ME is the not knowing. It is possible to worry endlessly about the variety of symptoms experienced and presume the worst. To live with this uncertainty for weeks is hard enough, to wrestle with it for years is intolerable. Good management in the early stages is essential if the illness is not to become chronic, but many sufferers have not been formally diagnosed for five, ten or even fifteen years. Is it any wonder that ME is so often self-diagnosed? As Richard Guest points out, 'It's strange, but when you have an unknown illness and then someone tells you the name for it, even though it's incurable, you're happy. You don't know how good it feels to have an answer after ten years not knowing.'[2]

Employment and ME

Many ME sufferers have carried on working, determined to 'beat this thing', but unfortunately this has resulted in them having the illness more severely than they might otherwise have done. Rest is essential in the early stages. Our society may applaud people who manage to keep going despite the odds, but ME is no respecter of this. Paradoxically, it is only as we learn to live within the boundaries of ME and not continually step outside them that the walls begin to expand.

It is essential that employers are informed about the nature of the illness from the beginning and can make the necessary plans to cover your absence. A letter from your doctor may be helpful even if ME hasn't been diagnosed yet. If ME has been diagnosed, a leaflet may put the employer more in the picture. Sufferers should be eligible for sick pay from their employers, but after this it is best to contact the Department for Work and Pensions (DWP). The DWP and the Department of Health both recognize ME as 'a disabling and distressing condition (with) a physical basis', and so state benefits are available, according to your level of disability. Some sufferers, however, still have to fight to receive these benefits.

Unfortunately, many sufferers have lost their jobs through ME, and trying to adjust to the limitations imposed as a result can be very difficult. For those who have been the main earners, the loss of prospects and income can be severe and a large mortgage may be impossible to maintain, forcing them to make yet more radical adjustments to their lifestyle.

Returning to work

Depending on the severity of the illness, you may want to explore the possibilities of part-time work. When you begin to feel better, it is very important that you don't push yourself to do too much too soon, as this can result in a relapse. It is therefore important to do less in practice than you think you can. If you feel you are up to returning to work for two days, try one day or even one morning and see how you get on.

When I had ME I was fortunate, because my headmaster and Local Education Authority were very supportive. Although I was wiped out for much of the first year, during the second year I was eased back on a very restricted timetable, teaching two mornings a week. As I seemed to be coping with this, the next term it was increased to a couple of days. Unfortunately, I had much more difficulty coping with my new timetable and began to relapse severely, and was then unable to return to school again. That period at work was very important because I began to feel like a 'normal' part of the human race again, but I'm not sure it was worth the high price I paid for it. When you are returning to work it is very important to balance what you might gain with what you could lose. Overstressing an already depleted system can result in another downward spiral, and it is better to progress very slowly than to be confronted with failure.

3

HOW CAN I HELP MYSELF?

No Hiding Place

I remember saying, when I had ME, 'I don't know who I am any more', so little did I resemble the person I had once been. Was my identity really so tied up in all that I did? Obviously it was. In fact, I used to dread having any time on my hands. Somehow I just had to keep busy, because that was productive and gave me a sense of achievement. Perhaps if I slowed down or stopped, I'd have to face the real me, which I knew wouldn't be a very pleasant experience.

Unfortunately, there is no hiding place in ME, because it strips away so much, and this is a very painful process. All you see is an increasing catalogue of things you can't do. It can feel as though some evil force has taken over your whole life and is painfully dismantling it in front of you. Everything is affected – and you are forced to surrender control. The mind becomes a battleground of negative thoughts fuelled by emotional instability, and soon it can seem as though you are imprisoned in a very dark tunnel with no escape route. It is then that there is a danger of the illness completely engulfing you. As my friend Deni wrote to me, 'I have ME, but I refuse to become the illness ME – I am still Deni!' It is quite a struggle to maintain your identity when ME affects so much of what you do and who you are. For many of us, our identity is bound up with what we do because our society tends to categorize us in this way, so having ME can make you feel a total misfit.

The Battle of the Mind

Unfortunately, we have a natural tendency to live in either the past or the future, spending little time in the 'now'. This can be counterproductive, because if my situation is dire now and I project negatively into the future, everything looks completely hopeless – there is no end to my dark tunnel. Equally, if I continue to look at all that I've lost and all that I once was, my current situation seems futile. If we can train our minds to live in the present it will help us to make the most of our situation now, rather than being robbed of everything. In the Bible, Jesus tells us not to worry about tomorrow, because 'each day has enough trouble of its own' (Mt. 6:34). This is very sensible advice for ME sufferers, who will probably need to divide the day into sections in order to get through it.

Negative scripts

We are what we think. Negative thinking is hard enough to counteract when you are well, but when you have ME it becomes a mighty battle. When your dreams, aspirations and hopes are shattered, when your body won't work for you, when you can't even maintain your house or look after your family, the frustration level rockets. The problem is that negative thinking produces negative feelings, which can then lead to negative actions. There is a domino effect, one negative thought leading to another until all the dominoes collapse. A typical negative script for ME might be this:

> Nobody believes me, nobody understands,
> nobody cares.
> I'm useless . . . valueless . . . worthless . . . unlovable.
> I'm a burden to others . . .
> Unwanted . . . alone.
> What's the point
> of living?

I think it can be reassuring to know how our minds tend to function. As I've been writing this book, I've had to continually fight to stop negative thoughts resurfacing and taking me captive. It was only as I wrote out the negative script for this situation that I could see how ridiculous it was and then became able to challenge it. The power of those thoughts then lost their grip.

> I won't be able to write the book . . . I'm not able to
> write the book.
> I'm not good enough . . . I'll let people down.
> I won't be able to make the deadlines.
> God will be disappointed with me.
> You're not meant to write the book.
> You're a failure
> to yourself,
> God and
> others.

What is interesting in this script is how the 'I's later change to 'You's, which are much more damning. It is as though I'm suddenly being accused and reprimanded by a powerful authority figure.

God is aware of the battle we face in our minds and that is why he tells us to 'be transformed by the renewing of your mind' (Rom. 12:2). He knows that it is a continual struggle for us, but it's one he longs to help us with. It is

32

only as we come to know the truth of our situation that we can challenge these negative thoughts and so change the script. As Jesus said, 'Then you will know the truth, and the truth will set you free' (Jn. 8:32).

ME Management

It is essential to manage ME before it manages you. There are choices to be made within ME which allow you to have some control over the illness, though it can seem to be like a game of snakes and ladders at times. As Dr Myhill explained to me when I was ill,

> Most ME sufferers compare themselves to what they were like before the illness began. This is hopeless. It is vital to find out exactly how much you can or can't do in a day without feeling ill the next day. You then do less.
>
> Imagine that a normal person has £1,000 worth of energy to spend in a day. The ME sufferer has only £100. This has to be spread out throughout the day in such a way that he or she has £20 change at the end. This will then allow for the recovery to take place. It usually takes at least one year and three relapses before this is fully understood. Relapses are not random and can nearly always be explained.

It is helpful to see the amount of energy we have in terms of money, as it help us to understand how we should spend or not spend our energy. I believe that it is important to use one small parcel of energy at a time. If we 'walk' slowly, we can reach the next small parcel of energy. However, if we 'run' for the big package, we risk exhaustion and possible relapse, and instead of progressing slowly forwards we begin to slide rapidly back. I tried to 'run' for the 'big' package in the second year of my illness and I ended up in a worse place than when I first developed ME. I know many other sufferers who have fallen into this trap. It is therefore essential that we not only allow our bank account to be in credit, but we also never go overdrawn. When we feel tempted to overdo things, it is important to remember how devastating it can be to be faced with further deterioration.

Like many sufferers, I have found the 75 per cent rule helpful. On any particular day, you only do 75 per cent of what you actually can do, rather than what you think you might be able to do. Then you see how your body responds over the next three days. Only doing one thing at a time and spacing these activities out is also important. As Action for ME comment in their excellent guidelines,

> Because ME tends to affect fit, healthy people who are enjoying their life and work, most people with ME find this advice very difficult. The typical pattern for someone with ME is: feel bad, rest a bit, feel a bit better, overdo it, feel worse for longer, rest a bit more, feel a bit better, overdo it again, feel much worse for much longer, etc. etc.

ME is a harsh teacher and many learn the lessons too late!

Rest

The single most important factor in recovery from ME is rest. There are various levels of rest, and it is important to have mental and emotional rest as well as physical rest. It is usually necessary to create boundaries so that you can protect that rest. You may be lying in bed, but if you are worrying about something, that is not true rest and uses a lot of energy. Equally, reading a book for a prolonged period of time or watching television may seem relaxing, but both activities require energy. Phone calls are a lifeline at times, but can completely wipe out an ME sufferer. They can be an utterly exhausting form of communication even for a well person, because of the intensity of concentration required. It is therefore important to limit the number and length of calls when you have ME, so as not to drain an already depleted energy reserve. An answering machine may be useful to screen your calls so that you have control over when and whether you ring the person back. Sending someone a note or an email can be less energy-consuming. I love receiving cards and letters because they are less intrusive than phone calls and I can then enjoy rereading them. They are also a much more permanent expression of what someone thinks or feels about you.

Few people really know how to rest and switch off. It is not something our culture encourages. Sometimes we need to be taught how to relax so that we can obtain the depth of rest that will aid recovery. Many sufferers have benefited from various relaxation techniques such as meditation or contemplative prayer. Contemplative prayer and meditation became a turning point in my own recovery from ME, but I shall explain more about this in Chapter 8.

Keeping a diary

It is very important to listen to your own body and to stay within your energy limits for each day. As Dr Anne Macintyre comments,

It was during the time that I was fighting against the weakness, and dragging myself about in an effort to keep going, that my condition deteriorated so fast and so permanently. As soon as I modified my life and listened to what my body was saying and kept within my limits whatever anyone said, it was amazing how the deterioration slowed down and almost stopped.[1]

This is where keeping a diary is useful. I found that writing very brief notes about my symptoms, how long I'd slept, what activities I'd done and for how long, was very helpful. I also rated the day out of ten and described it as 'good', 'bad' or 'the pits'! Keeping a diary helped me to become more objective about my illness and to see whether I was slowly improving or not. I began to see that it wasn't my 'bad' days that were the problem, because I was wiped out on those days: it was my 'good' days. I seemed to be at my most dangerous when I was having a 'good' day, because I would try to squeeze in too much and this would then set up a series of 'bad' and 'utterly awful' days. As a result of noticing this pattern, I tried to exercise some self-control on my 'good' days, though I found this very difficult to do.

These days, I keep a spiritual journal charting my ups and downs. I find this very beneficial as it helps me express my feelings to God about a particular situation or person and this in itself can be quite a releasing process. Very often it is a great encouragement to look back in my journal and see how situations that seemed impossible have changed. In many ways, I believe that it would have been helpful to keep a journal while I had ME.

Many sufferers, like modern-day psalmists, use poetry to express their anguish. Poetry is a very powerful medium for expressing emotions. The psalmists wrote from the pit of their despair, angry with God and crying out for him to do something about their situation. David Bridger expresses his feelings about ME in this poem:

> When you have suffered;
> when you have been in pain for years,
> when you are housebound,
> bedbound,
> bodybound;
> when you have accepted the fact
> that you don't appear on any statistics;
> when the only way you can express frustration
> is to write angry poetry
> which only your friends read;
> when the only thing you sign
> is the back of the page,
> so that someone can collect your benefit
> for you;
> when your pet poodle
> exhibits dominant behaviour
> towards you;
> sooner or later
> you reach the point
> where nothing scares you.

Why is This Happening to Me?

I believe that it is our 'Why?'s that take us on a journey into the heart of God. The question 'Why?' is essentially a spiritual question and there seems to be an increased hunger in our society for the spiritual. This was high-lighted after the death of Diana, Princess of Wales, and later by the shocking events of September 11th ('9/11'). The ongoing threat of terrorism has brought many of us face to face with our own mortality and the fragility of the human condition. Unfortunately no one escapes suffering. Jesus himself said that we would have trouble in this world (Jn. 16:33). Perhaps if we were able to accept the inevitability of this, we might find it easier to come to terms with our circumstances. My father made the same comment as TV personality Roy Castle when he discovered he had terminal cancer: 'Why *not* me?' I was staggered by his response and it still challenges me.

Although our 'Why?'s are important, they can concentrate our focus on the past and encourage introspection. Asking a different question can help to change our focus so that we can then move forward. It is more positive to focus on the *how* and the *what next*. Then we can begin to look at *how* to cope with our circumstances as well as consider *how* to get out of them.

Acceptance

Acceptance can become the key to unlock the ME prison. Accepting that you have ME is a positive step, as it allows you to get things into perspective and so get on with life. Acceptance can ultimately release us to see the positives rather than the negatives. If we dwell too much on our situation, it tends to focus us inwards, which is unhealthy. Making choices, however small, puts us in control. We may not have the choices we once had, but if we realize that we do still have power to choose and consciously act on those choices, we no longer feel like victims.

Acceptance is not the same as resignation. If I resign myself to having ME, it is as though I have given up and become a victim of the illness. I was continually having to come to terms with the changes in lifestyle initiated by

ME and so acceptance was not just a one-off decision, but a continuous process. After a considerable struggle, I learned to accept my illness and co-operate with the process. When I tried to fight ME physically, it beat me; such is the nature of the illness. I have found that when I ask God to come into the centre of my struggle, rather than insisting he remove it, my feelings begin to change. The level of acceptance in David's poem below is extraordinary considering that he has had ME severely for many years and is 100 per cent bedbound.

THE KEY

So, this is it Lord.
These are my circumstances;
This is my situation
You have ordained for me.
This is what I have to accept:

This pain;
This indignity;
This immobility;
This exhaustion;
This frustration.
So, this is my cup.

Thanks.

How can I not drink it?
How can I not bear it?
This is not my cross,
For I do not have a choice, do I?
Do I?

I cannot escape this pain,
This agony which sweats and tears
My dignity into shreds;
Which immobilizes me for years
And exhausts me beyond the pale;
Which rips my potential
Into shards.

This is not my cross
This is my situation.
Thanks.
Actually, yes, thanks.
Thanks for my situation,
For this is not my cross;
This is my key.

Thanks, Lord,
For changing my complaint
Into compliance.
Thanks for ridding me
Of my frustration and,
Please, do it again tomorrow.

Cheers!
Good health!
And, thanks again.

(David Bridger)

4

RELATIONSHIPS AND ME

A Process of Adjustment

If ME is hard for sufferers to understand and come to terms with, just imagine how difficult it must be for those who are close to you. It is essential, therefore, to give family and friends time to adjust to the 'new' you. People may not be able to respond immediately to your needs, but that doesn't mean they don't care.

Another problem is that there is a general lack of understanding about what it is like to suffer from ME. To make matters worse, ME sufferers often look better than they feel and so don't appear to be ill at all. It is difficult to explain that doing things which seem insignificant to others can have a profound effect on ME sufferers. Sometimes you simply have to say 'No' to people, which is not easy but is necessary to prevent a relapse. All these things can put a great deal of strain on a relationship.

Friendship

A friend of mine often says that communication oils the wheels of friendship, and she is right. Close relationships require a lot of maintenance. This is hard for an ME sufferer because of the peculiarities of the illness and the lack of energy. Part of the frustration of having ME is not being able to plan in advance, because you cannot predict how you are going to be. You soon discover who your real friends are. 'It soon sorts the wheat from the chaff,' as David explains, 'but I have made many new friends who I have "met" by phone and letter through our shared illness.' 'I have lost a few and some smile sceptically, which hurts!' says Hannah. 'I once forgot to meet up with a friend due to ME brain fog, and she didn't speak to me for two years!'

It is very important from the outset to explain to friends what you are going through and how ME is affecting you, so that they are prepared. Again you may find it helpful to give them a leaflet about the illness or refer them to a web site, to save yourself energy. We tend to expect people to be sensitive enough to know how we're feeling, but sometimes it is necessary to spell it out. As Steve comments, 'Most people, like myself, don't like to moan or to impose on people too much, but it is important not to suffer in silence, but to let people know how you feel. This helps to educate people so that they have a better understanding of what you're going through and have more realistic expectations.'

Expecting too much from our friends can also lead to disappointment. No one person can supply all our needs and so it is important to have realistic expectations, as people are bound to fail us at times.

Although many sufferers have been hurt by insensitive comments from friends, it is important to let go of that pain and appreciate the value of friendship. ME is an isolating illness and friendship can be a most precious gift.

To be without a friend is loneliness indeed! But what happiness, what security and joy to have someone with whom to speak confidently, as with another self, with whom to share all one's failures and success, and who can be trusted with the deepest secrets of one's heart.[1]

Being aware of our moods

It is important to be aware of our moods and feelings so that we can see how they may be affecting the people closest to us. When my desires are met, I tend to be happy, but when they are not, I can feel angry and frustrated. When I'm feeling particularly vulnerable through tiredness, illness or stress, I tend to misinterpret what people say and get very upset. When I am in this state, I am also more likely to see the bad in a person or situation rather than the good, and so become angry. Sometimes, my anger can be so blinding that I can't see any good in anything.

I recently found myself getting very upset with a close friend of mine. I was amazed by the anger that suddenly seemed to well up within me, fuelled by inner conflict and pain. Basically I felt hurt because my needs were not being met. My expectations of my friend, and my desires, did not take into account her needs and limited resources, and so there was a clash. This kind of incident must happen frequently in marriages, especially when one partner becomes more needy through illness. The conditions are then ripe for conflict.

I was alarmed at how quickly my anger turned to bitterness. As I tried to sleep that night, I continued to argue with my friend in my mind and pull up all the old resentments from the past. I tossed and turned, but the argument still raged. I was really shocked by what seemed to be surfacing from within me. As I tried to hand this situation over to God so that I could get some sleep, somehow the venom within me seemed to block my prayers.

I have come to realize that when my perspective of a situation is different to someone else's, there is the potential for an argument. It is only by continuing to talk things through that we can begin to understand each other's position and so find some neutral ground from which to proceed. On previous occasions when I have been wound up by what someone has said or done, I have been reminded of the words in Psalm 103, 'forget not all his benefits'. Although this scripture refers to God, it helps me to focus on the person's positive characteristics rather than dwell on the negative ones. It is as we begin to look at what a person really means to us, and all the ways in which they have shown their love, that we can begin to get things in perspective. Conflict does not have to be destructive; it can be the beginning of greater understanding and growth in any partnership.

Marriage

Unfortunately, ME can put a terrific strain on a marriage and if the marriage is already in difficulty that strain can be unbearable. As Mary writes, 'My husband said that one of the reasons that he left me was because of the ME. He couldn't handle it any longer. He said that I was no "fun" any more because I couldn't do a lot of the things we used to enjoy doing together.'

Mary has had ME for eleven years and as a result of her husband's comments she feels loaded with guilt. She has had to struggle with limited energy to bring up her daughter and help look after elderly parents. 'I should have tried to be a better wife, but I have such little energy and at times I have had to chose between my daughter and my husband.' The dreams they shared of owning a little cottage in the country are now being lived out with someone else. 'It hurts so much knowing that they are together and that he is sharing all our dreams with her. I suppose that is jealousy and is wrong, but it is just like a knife in my heart every time I hear that he is with her.'

Another sufferer, whom I met on retreat, writes, 'ME put an enormous strain on our marriage. At a time when we were drifting apart ME forced us to spend more time together. This year my husband and I shall be celebrating our silver wedding anniversary.'

It is very important that the partner tries to understand how the illness is affecting the sufferer, and so communication is essential. 'My husband has had to find within himself compassion. He is a scientist and believer in blind evolutionary forces, where survival of the fittest is the ultimate reality, and I think my illness has posed a challenge to that belief. I feel that God must be using my illness to bring about a change within him and I believe it is happening.' And Louise writes, 'My husband was a pain for a year, but once he understood more he was great.'

It was a real privilege for me to attend the marriage of a friend who has had ME since she was 18. It seemed as though she had lost all her future through ME, but at the age of 31 she met a wonderful man who was able to accept both her and the illness. I can't remember ever seeing her look so happy. I was particularly moved when they exchanged marriage vows, promising to love each other 'in sickness and in health'.

Coping with Children

Coping with children is a tall order when you have such limited energy. As Paula explains, 'There is a constant tension between my need for peace, quietness and rest, and the needs of an active family. Sometimes it feels as though I'm living in two worlds, the "well world" and the "ill world". I often pretend to live in the "well world", but know I'm not really one of them. I've had to learn to stop trying to protect them from the burden of ME and ask for help. Then I have valuable "well time" left over to spend in conversation with them and am able to meet some of their needs.'

Sarah writes:

In 1993 I was battling with the early stages of ME, not understanding what was going on and trying to cope with the demands of two growing children aged 4 and 7 and a husband who worked all hours. Those first three months were perhaps the hardest of all, in part due to my own determination to cope. I remember one evening, after taking the children to ballet, piano lessons and cubs, when I dropped my evening meal on the floor – I was so shaky with exhaustion I couldn't hold the plate. My husband just got cross with me; however, over the years he has become more understanding.

Time went on and I developed the pattern of good and bad times – I learned the hard way that doing too much on a good day meant more bad days to follow. I protected the children as much as I could, but there were inevitably times when I must have been very difficult to live with. My first trauma was having to cancel the family holiday to Disneyland in America which we had all been looking forward to. The following year we did get to France but I remember my 5-year-old saying to me, 'Mummy, I wish you didn't come on our holidays because you spoil them,' or words to that effect! I realized that she was looking at the situation logically through the eyes of a 5-year-old, but the hurt went deep just the same.

Once my daughter was at school full-time things got easier, but I still resisted an afternoon rest. Looking back I wished I'd listened to my body and less to my intellect. I thought that I could beat this thing and I developed tremendous willpower to keep going. It wasn't until this year that I finally accepted that my lifestyle had to change. I now have a regular sleep/rest in the afternoon, before the children come home from school, sometimes for two or three hours. The children have now accepted that I can't do what they and I would like to do.

Eileen expresses her pain and frustration through this poem:

I can't be the mother I want to be
with this pain, exhaustion, so little energy.
I'd love to jump in the pool, and swim with my son,
Splashing and laughing, having lots of fun.
When James is swimming, I sit on the side,
He wants me with him, I cry inside.

(Eileen McDonald Sayer)

One sufferer told me how she had found new hope and life since giving birth. 'It's given me such a positive new focus and such joy and happiness that even though I struggle to keep going, it's well worth it.' Another sufferer who has developed ME since having a baby feels that her son has almost sucked the life out of her. She thinks that she would make a far speedier recovery without him, but feels guilty for having these thoughts.

A dad with ME

Nick writes:

I had a fulfilling and demanding career until I got ill.
I provided well for my family and pretended I was
doing it all for them. The kids never wanted for
food, shelter or any other physical comfort. They
were never without love either, but it was my wife
who provided stability and continuity – I was rarely
around to do that. My brief spells at home tended to
be highlights for all of us, but often failed to live up
to expectations. Ours was a typical, high-stress,
make-it-up-as-you-go-along, naval family life.

I tried to keep up the old work routines after I got
ME and I collapsed into bed after two years and
stayed there. Those two years were hard for the
whole family; I was pretty stressed out and soft
targets are always the easiest. We all practised
target-practice on each other, but the kids and I have
grown out of that stage now.

I've got three daughters, now aged 15, 11 and 9.
The youngest can't remember a time when I was
healthy. The others remember my last year of
normal health, 1990 – which we spent in Gibraltar –
as a golden age. It was a good summer. I was in the
peak of fitness and I took a part-time volunteer job
as a lifeguard in the joint services open-air
swimming pool. I taught the kids to swim and they
watched me represent the Royal Navy in an inter-
service swimming gala just before we left the Rock.
That was probably the last time they felt proud of
their dad in any way that their school friends would
understand.

Our relationship now is comfortable and mellow.
I'm always there, even if I'm asleep. I'm around to

help them get their maths homework wrong and to listen to their problems and celebrations. I'm there to provide a buffer zone between them and their mum when she's reached the end of her tether or when they overstep the rebellion mark. I'm there to love them and to be loved, and it's great. Before I was ill I must have acted as though the kids were just small people who happened to live at my address; now we're good friends who really enjoy each other's company. I've learned more about life from my kids since I got ill than I learned in twenty years travelling the world and being important. Even if that was the only blessing God had bestowed on me through my illness, I would still be eternally grateful to him. My kids are a blessing to me, and I pray that I can be such to them. I couldn't have said that seven years ago!

(Help for those experiencing difficulties in their marriages or close relationships is listed in Appendix 3.)

Caring for an ME Sufferer

The following account by one sufferer highlights some of the problems faced by those who care for people with ME:

My wife's catchphrase is: 'I'm not a nurse, I didn't train to be one and I never signed up for this. I do my best and if you don't like it here go somewhere else.'

With my wife, what you see is what you get. I married her for that quality and I love her for it but I wouldn't have chosen her for a full-time carer – just as she certainly wouldn't have chosen me for a full-time invalid. Neither of us is suited to this position, yet God continues to keep us together, linked by a gossamer thread of mutual respect. When that respect is frayed, those are the times when we suffer.

My wife is permanently stressed, overworked and fed up. She is nurse, mother, housekeeper, accountant, gardener, odd-job woman, decorator, vet's assistant (for two dogs and a tank of fish), and has a million other jobs. She is a perfectionist with no chance of doing all these jobs perfectly, so is always frustrated. I'm the obvious cause of this unhappiness. Most of all, she is a prisoner and considers me – not my illness but me – her jailer. She tends to equate care with control and when I resist this control she interprets it as a rejection of the whole care package, and of herself.

A difference in perspective

When someone you love becomes ill you each view your life together from different perspectives. The natural reaction is to want to put things right – to try and fix it. Unfortunately this can sometimes lead to a head-on collision. If carers try to do too much for the sufferer and so take away their already limited control and independence, this can further damage their fragile self-esteem. So carers have to learn the hard lesson of allowing sufferers to do things their way and to make mistakes. Living with ME is a steep learning curve for both sufferer and carer and so both parties need to be allowed to make mistakes. Good communication is essential.

What is the carer going through?

I've heard it said that the worst form of suffering is to watch someone you love suffer and not be able to do anything about it. One of the hardest things for the carer to face is the permanency and extent of the person's disability. A carer may feel they have been robbed of a wonderful wife, husband or child, and that in itself is hard to come to terms with. In this loss, it is not uncommon for a carer to go through a similar grieving process to the sufferer, experiencing denial, bargaining, anger, depression and acceptance. Carers can also feel like victims robbed of choice.

Being a carer can put an enormous strain on other relationships in the family too, so that it becomes impossible to either give to or receive from them. It is essential that carers are able to let off steam in an appropriate way and have a break from the situation. It is important to let those close to them know what they need so that they can help share the load. Carers also need to maintain their own life as far as they can, though this may be nearly impossible in some cases. Carers cannot keep giving and giving without renewing their own energy and strength in some way, so it is important to plan in things to look forward to as well as breaks away. (Help for carers and other useful information is listed in Appendix 3 at the back of this book.)

5

WHAT SUFFERERS SAY ABOUT ME

Living With ME

Jackie writes, 'It is very difficult coming to terms with a prospective long-term illness; the continual roller coaster of relapse and remission is devastating. Loss of control, dignity, especially in communication, and the inability to perform certain ever-changing tasks is confusing and, at times, frightening. For example, today I cannot do what I was able to do yesterday; perhaps tomorrow I shall do twice as much, or nothing at all!'

Approximately 25 per cent of ME sufferers are severe sufferers. I was given a disturbing insight into this world when one sufferer wrote to me,

My body is wrecked: I'm almost totally bedbound, to the extent that I'm reduced to using a bed-bottle and cannot trust myself to lift it out of the bed when I'm done. I'm sweating a nasty corrosive oily substance which burns my skin all the time and I'm incapable of climbing into a bath.

My carer is out of action: my wife slipped a disc and trapped a nerve some weeks ago and is absolutely forbidden to bend or stretch or do any of the things she normally does to help me. I phoned Social Services and a care worker now comes in every morning to give me a bed bath. I now have my own Care Manager who came to assess my needs and told me, regretfully, that her care workers couldn't lift me into the bath because I have no hoisting equipment (Health and Safety), so she arranged an occupational therapy assessment. I should receive my hoist soon and am on a three-year waiting list for a stair lift. Meanwhile I haven't had a bath for the last six weeks, and a long soak in a hot bath is my normal form of pain relief, so my muscles are now rock hard and permanently cramped. I got round the greasy hair problem by getting one of my kids to borrow a pair of hair clippers and give me a 'number one', so now my bed bath includes a scalp scrub!

In the following section sufferers share what it is like to live with ME. They talk openly about their hopes, fears, pain and frustration.

What are your worst fears?

- *Never living again.*
- *I used to fear that I would never recover.*
- *That I will have to look after my elderly parents.*
- *Now I'm over 70, life must deteriorate anyway. My husband is 77 and my worst fear would be having to live without him.*
- *I used to be afraid that I was going mad and that I would be taken into a mental home.*
- *That I'll get worse and become more dependent and immobile.*
- *I prefer not to focus on any fears. I try not to give way to any negative thoughts.*
- *That my daughters will inherit a genetic vulnerability to ME.*
- *I fear being left alone.*

- *Being a burden on my family.*
- *I feared I was going to die.*

What are the hardest aspects of the illness to cope with?

One frustration for sufferers is that well people do not generally understand the difference between temporary fatigue due to overwork and the chronic disabling fatigue they are experiencing. Comments like 'Oh, I feel like that' completely undermine the sufferer and invalidate their illness. Here are some other things sufferers have told me they find it difficult to cope with:

- *Other people's lack of understanding.*
- *People saying you look well when you feel utterly awful.*
- *Not being able to do the things I want to do.*
- *Memory lapses. Mental exhaustion. No life.*
- *Loss of career. Loss of social life.*
- *Being unable to help others.*
- *Emotional instability. The inability to absorb information.*
- *Just never feeling well.*
- *Not being able to plan ahead, and if I try to, having to cancel at the last minute because I'm not well enough.*
- *Knowing that I am putting extra pressure on other members of the family.*
- *The hurt of being forgotten is almost as painful as the illness itself.*
- *The unknown. ME's unpredictability.*
- *Frustration and a loss of self-worth until I accepted the redundancy of my old set of values.*
- *The wasted years that can never be reclaimed, even if I'm healed.*
- *Letting people down.*
- *Looking back I had high hopes that in a few months I'd be better, but as the years go by those hopes diminish.*

• *The isolation and loneliness.*

How do you keep going?

Many sufferers in this and the following section mention the importance of their faith in God, despite their apparent struggle for survival. This is how they cope:

• *Not feeling sorry for myself and finding a purpose to get out of bed each day.*
• *Trusting in God's provision. Knowing that he will meet all my needs.*
• *The love of God and friends.*
• *Faith and prayer. But when I'm very low I can't pray.*
• *I set a goal/aim for each day but try to remember the 75 per cent rule.*
• *By developing activities that can be done sitting down, e.g. painting, writing poetry.*
• *Meeting as a prayer group with other Christians with ME has been invaluable.*
• *My love for my family and my trust in God and hope for healing.*
• *I don't always. My husband is a great help and encouragement to me. I'm sure prayer and being prayed for helps.*
• *There's really no option. It was harder at the beginning because I wouldn't ask for or accept help. Prayer helps a lot.*

Are there any positive things that have happened during your illness?

Here's what some people experienced as positives:

• *I've made some new friends who are ME sufferers.*
• *I think it has brought me closer to God and made me realize*

> *how totally dependent I am on him.*
- *I've spent more time with my husband.*
- *I've had to stop rushing around and learned how to relax.*
- *It's given me the opportunity to learn computer skills.*
- *I write poetry and I've learned to play the violin. I have also developed several ME poetry-writing groups.*
- *I have drawn closer to God and the creative side of me is being drawn out in paintings, poems and pottery.*
- *Finding the 'treasures in darkness'.*
- *Good ME friends.*
- *Starting an ME prayer group.*
- *Knowing that my husband loves me in spite of everything is such a blessing.*
- *I have much more empathy for others suffering illness and am more sensitive to their needs.*
- *Meeting people who have been healed of ME.*
- *I became a Christian through ME.*
- *I met my husband.*
- *I've been partially healed and have since become a Christian.*

What advice would you give other ME sufferers that may be helpful?

Sufferers are in the best place to advise others on how to cope with the illness and so in this section they share their thoughts:

- *Learn to 'be' rather than to 'do'. Be a Mary not a Martha.*
- *Accept the limitations ME places on you and live within them. People do recover from ME eventually. There is hope.*
- *Try to develop activities that you can do.*
- *Try to express your feelings that can so often become crushed down inside, through words, pictures or song.*
- *Never lose hope. Try not to mourn daily for what you used to be, accept what is and take one day at a time.*

- *Let go and let God help you.*
- *Listen to your body, not to the advice of others.*
- *Accept help when it is offered. If you keep refusing it makes it more difficult to ask for help when you really need it.*
- *Go to a qualified alternative medical practitioner.*
- *Do as much as you can and leave the rest. Set small attainable goals each day and don't blame yourself.*
- *Be very open with others.*
- *Try to get some fresh air regularly.*
- *Talk to other sufferers.*

'All in the Mind'

I don't believe people have any idea of the devastating effect that the words 'all in the mind' have on a sufferer. As one sufferer commented, 'disbelief crucifies trust', and this damages relationships and further isolates a sufferer. Our society is unfortunately quick to judge, to label and to categorize. It is probably something we are all guilty of over different issues, but with ME there is often such polarisation of opinion that it sets up two opposing beliefs – 'mental' or 'physical' – which inevitably leads to further conflict as people defend and argue their positions.

ME carries an 'all in the mind' stigma because its cause cannot yet be clearly defined. Also, because depression is so often a symptom of ME, it tends to be put in the category of a mental illness. Other illnesses, including Multiple Sclerosis, have been labelled this way in the past. It seems that if no physical cause can be found for an illness it is automatically labelled psychological! Illness or injury affects our whole system, not just our body. To argue over whether an illness is 'mental' or 'physical' makes little sense because it denies the fact that we are triune beings – body, soul and spirit – and so what happens to our body is bound to affect the rest of us.

Depression can be a symptom of ME, or simply a natural result of adjusting to any long-term medical disorder. Labelling ME sufferers as depressed and denying the organic nature of the illness is ridiculously simplistic. I received extensive physiotherapy at an NHS unit, and although my physical needs were attended to, I was screaming out in pain emotionally and spiritually. My damaged knee was affecting the whole of me, and at one point, when everything seemed hopeless, I had to really struggle not to enter the pit of depression. This is not 'all in my mind'; it is a natural response to injury, disablement and loss. I think one of the reasons why alternative therapies are so popular is that they avoid such categorisations and aim to treat the whole person.

Many people's judgement of ME is based on lack of knowledge and understanding. They have not spent time with a sufferer on a daily and weekly basis and so do not see the whole picture. Doctors and consultants are quick to label and to pigeonhole this illness. A more flexible and open-minded attitude and willingness to constructively discuss this illness and listen to sufferers would lead to considerable progress being made. Sufferers would then feel less condemned by instant judgements.

I believe it is a fundamental human right for everyone to be believed. Someone in the medical profession recently told me that although she now believed that God could heal people, she couldn't believe in my healing because she didn't believe in ME. All the patients she has seen were depressed; therefore in her mind ME and depression are the same. It was hard for me not to feel the sting of this comment, but I lived through the reality of ME and know how privileged I am to have been released from it. God healed me instantly, and as a friend who is a doctor pointed out, 'People don't get better instantly from either depression or ME.' I believe that God must be angered by the injustices of this illness. In the end, sufferers have little choice but to forgive the cutting comments of others, because to hold on to them puts further stress on an already depleted system.

What Doctors with ME Say About ME

Linda, who used to be a GP before her illness, wrote:

> During my time as a GP I learnt a lot about people and how they cope with all sorts of problems. I then became ill with ME and am still struggling with the physical, mental, emotional and social disabilities which have resulted from it. Some directly due to how the illness affects me, others due to our society's attitudes. Coping on my own in the face of a mixture of prejudice, ignorance and judgemental responses from both 'caring' professionals and friends, has added considerably to the difficulties.

Dr Charles Shepherd is Medical Advisor to the ME Association, and suffers with ME. He explains why he took up this post:

> The main reason I took up the challenge stems from personal experience of living with ME. Having contracted an extremely severe fatigue syndrome following an attack of chicken pox several years ago (caught, incidentally, from one of my patients), I

soon began to appreciate all the physical, social and psychological problems that this wretched illness drags along with it. I also became acutely aware of how little support or good practical advice was being offered by doctors at this point in time. Fortunately, the position has started to change for the better, but we still have a long way to go and a lot of minds to change.[1]

Dr Anne Macintyre, former medical adviser to the ME Association, has written an excellent book on ME (see Appendix 1). It is written for the benefit of other sufferers, carers, friends and relations, as well as for doctors who still do not believe that ME is a genuine disease. In the introduction she begins by describing her own story:

My own story is a typical example. Five years ago I was able to work full-time in a busy hospital department and spend my free time gardening, decorating an old house, socializing and generally living a full life . . .

Four years ago, during a spell of very hard work while in India, I had a severe throat infection, but had to carry on working. After I returned home I remained unwell and tired for many weeks. Over the following three years I had periods of severe exhaustion alternating with short spells of nearly normal energy.

I had bouts of unexplained depression and feelings of utter 'awfulness', when I felt more ill than at any previous time in my life. I had to cut down my work to part-time and rest when not working. In the past I had found that a long walk in the countryside, or a swim, would lift me out of 'the blues'. But now, any exercise was having a disastrous effect, and I had more benefit just spending a weekend in a chair. I knew that something was wrong, but no one could identify it. I feared that I was very neurotic or maybe losing my mind.

Then a flu-like illness, which featured fever and terrible muscle pains, seemed to plunge me into a worse state. Over the following three months, I became unable to walk 50 yards without collapsing; my brain turned into cotton wool. I was unable to read or bear the sound of music, weird symptoms plagued me, including waking in the night with palpitations and loud noises in my head, my vision was often blurred, I smelt things that were not there. But the overriding problem was the extreme exhaustion brought on by the simplest task, even brushing my hair, or chopping some vegetables.[2]

Dr Macintyre later comments that 'ME is a diagnosis based on the history of a patient's illness', rather than any single diagnostic test, and that 'the only branch of medicine that does not depend on tests or abnormal physical findings is psychiatry, and it is into this pigeon-hole that many ME patients are put'.[3]

Dr Clare Fleming wrote an interesting article in 1994 in the *British Medical Journal* entitled 'The Glass Cage', describing her experience of ME:

I live in a glass cage. Often I seem to be well, so only those close to me see the extent of my disability. Indeed, within my prison of inactivity, there are moments when I feel relatively well. Yet the invisible walls around me are impenetrable. Beyond them lies a barrage of symptoms and the further I push myself, the longer the recovery time: hours, days, even weeks.

My cage is myalgic encephalomyelitis, one of the chronic fatigue syndromes. I was a general practitioner when the first symptoms appeared three years ago, shortly after I was immunized against hepatitis B. The following month I developed glandular fever and my illness began in earnest, with multiple symptoms, which continually varied in intensity: sore throat, swollen glands, fatigue, 'brain fog', malaise, myalgia, muscle fatigue, fasciculation, sweats, postural hypotension, alcohol intolerance, poor memory, emotional lability, and loss of atopic response.

Words can lie comfortably on a page, distanced by medical terminology. But this list invaded my life. . . At first I fought the symptoms, attempting to overcome the disease by positive thinking and sheer determination. After nine months of setbacks and fruitless struggle I was drained to the point of feeling death would be a relief. I sank into depression, a disorientating experience quite different from other stages of the illness. This rapidly passed with treatment.

Medical training had not equipped me to understand myalgic encephalomyelitis.[4]

Reaching Out to ME Sufferers

ME sufferers feel desperately alone in this illness and long for friendship. As one sufferer writes, 'Sometimes I need the freedom to express honestly what I'm struggling with, without judgement and pat answers.' No one can fully identify with what another is going through, but to be listened to is a real gift for a sufferer and can be very healing in itself. During the time of my knee injury, I really appreciated those friends who offered practical help without me asking. I also really enjoyed 'special treats' like being taken to the theatre or cinema and being invited round for a meal. When a person has to spend so much time in their home, going out is a wonderful luxury and something to look forward to.

What would you like well persons to know?

American sufferers made the following comments in response to this question on the Internet:

- *We want well people to know that we want to socialize but sometimes we can't handle a phone call. Please don't take it personally but call again.*
- *Understand that our symptoms vary from hour to hour as different systems in our bodies become affected. What is happening today might be superseded by other symptoms tomorrow.*
- *When our memory shuts down, it doesn't mean that what you said isn't important to us; our brains just didn't register at that moment.*
- *I'm still the same person; I just don't have the abilities I used to.*
- *When you see us out on an errand and say, 'You look wonderful, you must be all better now,' we feel like you don't realize that we may have just used up our entire energy quotient for the day and will probably drop in bed when we get home.*
- *I'm able to do a lot if I do it at my own pace.*
- *It means a lot when you include us in your social events and don't get offended when we can't make it.*

6

YOUNG ME

Loss of Childhood

Research published in 1997 by Jane Colby and Dr Elizabeth Dowsett showed that 51 per cent of the children who could not attend school for a year or more had ME.

Unfortunately, children have to suffer the injustices of ME too. Many paediatricians do not believe in ME, and so children have been labelled as 'school phobic' or 'hypochondriac'. It is also much harder for children to articulate how they feel and to describe their fluctuating symptoms.

I don't think any of us can fully appreciate what it must be like to have ME when you are a child or young adult. The isolation, loneliness, loss of childhood, loss of friends and peers, of qualifications, hobbies, interests, independence, career prospects etc – the whole of life seemingly slipping away, with little in the future to look forward to.

Several young sufferers in this chapter offer an insight into their world.

Peter

Peter is aged 10 and has had ME for seven months:

> My illness started with flu-like symptoms and I suffer with migraines, earache and vertigo. I have severe headaches day and night. I can only walk on

my knees. I feel very tired and down and very frustrated that I can't walk about.

I really miss seeing my friends, going for walks, playing my violin and playing tennis. I used to love going swimming too. I have only one good friend left. We've had a new cat called Millie and I like playing with her and listening to music.

I'm just hoping I'll get better soon. I don't like to think about what could happen to me, I just take one week at a time. The worst thing that has happened to me is listening to doctors who say my illness is 'all in the mind'.

ME often prevents young people from attending school and enjoying normal activities like going to the cinema and pursuing hobbies. They often lose the opportunity to make new friends, enjoy an active social life and explore 'who they are'. If they are unable to attend school for several years, they may lose contact with their friends altogether and feel totally isolated. The physical, emotional and psychological suffering of these youngsters can be acute.

Emma

Emma was a pupil at my school and became ill when she was 12. Her story highlights many of the problems experienced by young ME sufferers. What follows is a transcript of a recording she made for a school assembly I was taking on ME:

I am 15 years old and for the past three-and-a-half years I feel like I've been existing rather than living. I've got the illness ME. It started at the age of 12 when I had suspected glandular fever. I am now unable to walk around the garden without a walking stick or my parents to help. I can't go further than a few yards and if I do go out I have to have a wheelchair. I have terrible pain in all my muscles, especially my back and legs, and I am never without a headache. Sometimes I get very depressed, but I know that my depression is caused by ME.

Even though I am ill, I carry on my education. I have a home tutor called Val who's excellent and she helps me to get through my very lonesome days. I'm taking my GCSEs, all being well, next year. Val is like a best friend to me and even though she is older than me she can help give me an experience of what it is like to be young.

I'm completely missing out on life. I can't go to school and there is so much more to education than just the different subjects; it's the growing-up part of education as well. I know that when I am older I can catch up with my friends, but I know that I will never be able to have the experience of my first year, my second year, my third year, my fourth year and it very much looks like my fifth year at school. I've had one term at senior school and that just hasn't given me the experience I need to grow up. I know what it is like to feel pain, but I don't know what it is like to go to the cinema and go out with friends.

I find the isolation very difficult to cope with. I'm on my own practically all the day except when my home tutor comes, and I know that on the odd day when I have been on my own I've been very depressed. My mind wants to do things. It wants to make a card, write a letter, do some sewing, do some cookery; but my body is physically not able to. My muscles are very weak and I am tired all the time.

It's very difficult for other people to understand what it is like. I feel like I'm in prison. My body is a prison and I can't get out of it. The germs inside just keep on ruining and overruling my body, and at the moment I feel that I'm worse than I've ever been throughout my illness. There have been worse patches, though, when I have had a relapse, which is when I can't get out of bed, I can't move and I have to be fed. Luckily, these very serious relapses don't happen too often.

I feel like I want to get out but I can't. I feel like I want to run away, but physically and mentally I can't do that, as my legs won't carry me. They hardly carry me around the house, so I dread to think what it would be like to get to the bus stop or just the shops down the road. I have to limit the times I go up and downstairs. I crawl up the stairs and come down on my bum. I have a certain amount of energy a day and that is centred around my school work. The rest of the time I spend in bed. That's basically how I fill my time – very entertaining! I don't know what I'd do without my work.

I sometimes see myself singing on stage or playing tennis and doing normal things, but the truth is, I can't really remember what it is like not to be in pain. I've had a headache now for three-and-a-half years and I can't remember what it is like to run. If I could be told when I'd get better, even if it was two or three years' time, I'd be happy and could and would start planning my life.

Some time later, Emma wrote to me about her examination experience:

The exam boards have been understanding and allowed me to sit the exams at home, with supervision from school. So for two weeks in June our dining room was turned into the 'examination room'. To be truthful, I have absolutely no idea how I managed to take them. I had eight exams in ten days and I'm sure I must have been running on autopilot! I think about it now and can't remember it clearly, almost as though I was unconscious. My results come out in August and whatever I get will be a bonus and I will have achieved the results. Maybe they won't be as good as if I was at school, but at least I will have managed to get something out of the last five years, instead of just thoughts, most or all of them unpleasant about my illness.

Courage

A testimony to Emma's courage and perseverance is that she gained eight GCSEs, three at grade A and five at grade B. Educationally, Emma was fortunate. She is a bright and capable youngster who has benefited from the close co-operation between the school and her home tutor. She has not had to struggle to gain the necessary hours of home tuition, which I know has been a problem for many young sufferers. Members of staff have visited her at home at regular intervals to ensure the continuity of her course work.

However, while her classmates entered the sixth form the following September, Emma remained at home struggling to cope with the demands of A-levels. Her classmates, though sympathetic to her condition, can now hardly remember her.

The limitations imposed by ME meant that it has taken Emma six years to complete three A-levels because she only has the energy to cope with one at a time. She has gained A-levels in mathematics, physics and biology and is applying to various universities. Emma is now 21 and whereas her peers will be leaving university having completed their degrees, she is just beginning the application process. Unfortunately, unless she is able to negotiate special arrangements and conditions with a particular university, she may well have to come to terms with the fact that she is not well enough to study for a full-time degree and may have to consider a part-time degree instead. Facing up to this possibility is difficult because, like other young ME sufferers, she longs to have some normality in her life and to be doing things others her age are doing.

The 'Good News'

Most young sufferers do improve gradually and make a full recovery. Many have also been miraculously healed of this illness.

Lisa, another former pupil from my school, developed ME so badly that she became totally bedbound and spent all her time in a darkened room. At times, she was unable even to feed herself. Her mother had to give up her job as a teacher to look after her. After many years, however, she was healed through attending a week of worship and ministry with Sozo Ministries. Her mother sent me this letter shortly afterwards:

> We travelled to Devon with Lisa lying on a mattress in a darkened Renault Espace. She was still virtually paralysed and in constant pain. We brought her home sitting up in the front of the car.
>
> Since September 1991, we have been revelling in the renewal of our family life as Lisa walked into her

healing. She has progressed through three wheel-chairs, crutches and walking sticks, and now walks unaided. It is a mixture of a John McCarthy release and a new baby. We are thrilled. She swims regularly, shops, goes out walking and is always busy reading, writing or sewing. It has been miraculous. She radiates good health as she radiates Jesus.

Kathryn, formerly a severe sufferer, has written a wonderful autobiography about her life with ME called *Kathryn's story*.[1] Kathryn was healed when a lady called Sue from her church prayed for her. Sue felt that God had told her that he would heal Kathryn of ME. She felt what she describes as a real 'burden' for Kathryn and knew that she was meant to pray for her. Kathryn was subsequently healed.

How ME Affects Families and Friendships

Kathryn offers a very revealing insight into this area in her book. She writes:

At first my dad found my illness and disability difficult to accept. It was as if he felt embarrassed about the way I walked and the fact that I was so ill. When we got the wheelchair he wasn't keen to take me out in it and that really used to annoy me because the only time I could get out of the area was when he was at home with the car. When he did get used to it, though, he was brilliant and gradually took me out more and more.

It was difficult, too, for Alison [Kathryn's sister]. At school she had to put up with people saying that her sister was a 'spastic'. Her friends didn't help by saying things like, 'ME? Don't you die of that?' She even thought we might be hiding the fact that I was going to die, when of course we weren't, because I wasn't!

Sisters always argue. During my illness we still did, but in a slightly different form. Alison got jealous because I seemed to be getting more attention than she was, and I got angry with her because she could do all the things I couldn't – and still complained. Despite the arguments, though, we loved each other and didn't like to see the other hurting.

Then there was Mum, who really bore the brunt of my illness. Fortunately she didn't go out to work in the day, and so was at home to look after me ... Through my illness I was dependent on Mum, as a small child would be. She walked miles, pushing me in the wheelchair; and when I did walk a short distance, I leaned on her ... Of course we had our arguments and I sometimes used to feel stifled being with her so much. She probably felt the same about me, but without her I don't know how I would have coped.

When you are ill, particularly for a long time, you find out who your real friends are. . . . As time went by, though, the numbers of visitors thinned out. . . . Despite studying for GCSEs, Rebecca found time to visit me every week. I was grateful for that because she was a contact with the goings-on at school. It can't have been easy for her. Some weeks I must have seemed very quiet and depressed, but she stuck by me.[2]

At university

One young sufferer whom I knew of when I was ill, and who has had ME for ten years, found that he gradually got better after his first year at university and is now coping well with the demands of his degree.

Sarah told me her story when she was finishing the final year of her degree. I believe that it highlights some of the issues facing young ME sufferers at this important stage in their lives.

I became ill with a flu-like virus, during the summer of 1990, just before I was due to start my degree in History. I was 18 years old. I battled my way through those first weeks at university, but simply ended up in bed. I think I spent most of my first year asleep. I kept going to the university doctors, but they kept saying, 'It's just stress and the pressure of being away from home.' At the beginning of the second year of my degree, I got out of bed one day and suddenly found that I couldn't walk or vocalize any words. My parents came to take me home and the doctor diagnosed post-viral fatigue syndrome and told me that I would recover after six weeks' complete rest. I was bedbound and so ill that my parents had to look after me. It was one-and-a-half years before I tried to return to begin the second year of my degree again.

I managed to get through my second year of university with the help of my friends who took notes for me and through taking an increasing number of painkillers. I had chronic fibromyalgia and was experiencing pain in all my muscles and joints as well as associated nerve pain. The ringing in my ears was constant and the fatigue enveloping.

I could now no longer write. I attempted to go into my third year, but had to drop out. My department's attitude was effectively to tell me to go away until I got better. It would have helped me if the university had had a learning support unit that catered for special needs.

During my second attempt to return to university to complete my third year, I stumbled across information on the disabled students' allowance. This allowance allowed me to have people come in as note-takers as well as have a specially adapted computer. I could no longer use the mouse on the computer because of the pain in my hands and so it was loaded with a specially adapted program. I don't know how I would have coped without this special help. I am now just about to complete my degree, my last year having taken four years, and the whole degree eight years!

It unnerves me that I'm now actually 26 and about to graduate. I feel I should be 21, and in fact, I feel as though I were 58! People all around me are getting on with their lives and I seem to be achieving so little so very slowly. I'm living on painkillers and I'm worried about being 'written off' from the job market. Other people seem to be beginning their careers and yet some of my friends probably don't even think I'm interested in getting a job because I've had to take so much time out of university.

In the future I'd like to facilitate disabled access into education. I've had to fight every step of the way to get the help I've needed. I'm not asking for special treatment, just the specialized help and equipment I need so that I can begin from the same starting point as everyone else.

My priority now is to rest and recover from my degree, but I'm worried about what comes next. Am I well enough to hold down any kind of job, or would any employer want to take me on? Some people assume that I'm just a 'slacker', which is very offensive when you're in so much pain.

I can only be real about my illness with a core of people I trust. Other people simply can't handle it. I've had friends, but they've got jobs now. Others at university simply saw me as a 'party pooper' and grew tired of me being ill. I'm wary of male relationships because I don't want to inflict my illness on them. It's tough enough for me to cope with.

Sarah successfully completed her university course and graduated, but not without a severe struggle which not everyone in her position can manage. Students like Sarah need considerable courage, determination and endurance to be able to live with the devastating effects ME has on their lives.

7

OUT OF THE DEPTHS

Emotions

I don't believe there is any easy answer to the emotional havoc that ME creates. There is nothing wrong with having these emotions; it is what we do with them that is important. The problem comes when we let our emotions rule and control us. When this happens, the truth and reality of our situation can be obscured.

I find it reassuring to know that God understands our emotions. He created us as emotional beings and so appreciates the problems we face. God allowed his Son to enter this world as a baby so that he could identify with the fragility and vulnerability of our human condition. Jesus was born into poverty and became 'despised and rejected by men, a man of sorrows, and familiar with suffering' (Is. 53:3). He freely displayed his emotions, weeping at the death of his friend Lazarus, and, nailed to a cross, cried out, 'My God, my God, why have you forsaken me?' (Mk. 15:34). It seems our culture has a 'hang-up' about people expressing their emotions (unless it is on a football pitch!) and yet our emotions are a natural expression of who we are.

A kind of bereavement

Some years ago, I lost someone I cared about very much, a woman I knew better than anyone in the world. For a couple of years the grief was so intense and I mourned intensely. Slowly the grief eased and there were only moments when something reminded me of her and the pain returned just as sharply. Now I can think of her calmly and with affection, and be glad that I had the experience of knowing her. I get a pang from time to time, but it is usually a fairly mild one – nothing like the agony of the first years. What I haven't mentioned is that the woman I mourned for was myself, the person I used to be before I got ME.

Becoming chronically ill is very much like a bereavement. The losses and the emotions involved are very similar. Having to give up a job I loved meant that I lost income, status, companionship and an acknowledged role, the same kind of things I would have lost if I had been widowed. I have wept for all the things that I will probably never do again; I have ached for the companionship I once had; I have felt guilty about the lifestyle that perhaps made me more vulnerable. Most of all though, I have been angry – with myself and with other people.[1]

ME tends to spotlight the full range of a person's emotions and magnify them out of all proportion. Sometimes it can feel as though you are wrestling with a monster. As Dr Myhill commented to me, 'A doctor can help with the physical management of the illness through advice, supplements and different forms of alternative regimes, but in the end it is down to the person. They have to sort out and confront the spiritual and emotional side of the illness. Confronting the skeletons in the cupboard is an incredibly painful process and takes a lot of courage.'

Sorting out the spiritual and emotional part of the ME jigsaw is a considerable challenge. It is much easier to hide away from the world with ME than to face all the painful but life-giving steps that lead to wholeness. But it is only as we come to terms with these issues that we can learn to live both within and beyond the apparent confines of ME and for the walls of what seems like a prison to be expanded.

The problem of pain

It is easy to forget how debilitating and energy-sapping pain is. I suffered a severe relapse when my knee suddenly 'clunked'. This resulted in the most excruciating pain. Lying there for what seemed like an eternity, unable to do anything, reminded me of my own powerlessness. We take the control we have over our bodies so much for granted, but when they seem to mutiny, fears can overwhelm and thoughts of despair creep in as we see our freedom slowly slipping away from us. When I am in pain, I feel exposed, raw and vulnerable. My body then feels like a prison. I'm trapped inside a painful body that won't work for me. Then I begin to feel trapped by my surroundings too. I become irritable and short-tempered and I feel like lashing out at someone.

Experiencing pain can be such a lonely and isolating experience because it seems that nobody understands how we feel. Time seems endless, the walls seem to close in and a thick blanket of darkness descends. Enduring long periods of isolation can result in a numbing loneliness that affects not only the mind but the spirit too.

With pain comes fear and panic. I developed a new pain lower down my leg, which threw me into great anxiety. I said to myself, 'Oh, great! This injury is spreading down the rest of my leg now, is it?' I was angry with God and with myself. It reminded me of a very telling comment one ME sufferer made while I was in South Africa. She said, 'I've got past the stage where every new pain represents a new fear.' Clearly I had not reached that stage with my knee!

When I'm in pain, I long to be comforted, and if there is no one to comfort me, this accentuates my feelings of loneliness and isolation. I struggle to feel God's 'everlasting arms' encircling me, because what I really want is 'arms with flesh' that comfort and reassure me, and say, 'Hush, my child, everything is going to be OK. I'm here for you.' Sometimes it can feel like God has abandoned me. David, the psalmist, expressed this feeling very powerfully in Psalm 13:1–2:

> How long, O LORD? Will you forget me for ever?
> How long will you hide your face from me?
> How long must I wrestle with my thoughts
> and every day have sorrow in my heart?
> How long will my enemy triumph over me?

Jane Grayshon, a writer who has lived with severe pain for many years, comments:

> Yet it is in those worse moments that we can stumble almost accidentally upon heaven, where it is least to be expected.
> Or is it? I am beginning to wonder if this is where heaven is most to be expected . . . when we are past coping, where there is nothing left of ourselves – nothing left that we can do, or give or even be.
> And then God steps in.[2]

It is out of the depths that I have literally cried out to God to heal my knee. It is the cry of feeling utterly alone and yet somehow trusting in a God who longs to heal and restore.

Fear

The difference between worry and fear is that fear has a focus. Fear strangles freedom and is a particularly difficult emotion to deal with. Sometimes I find that fear creeps up on me for no apparent reason. It may be totally irrational and unfounded, but once I've faced that particular fear, it represents another battle won.

Many of us have a variety of deep-seated fears. One of these may be the fear of rejection and the root of that fear may take some time to uncover. We all long to be liked, loved, encouraged, accepted and affirmed. However, ME can set up a fear of rejection, as our self-image is based on what others think of us and often that is based on what we 'do'. We may even hold up other people's opinions as a mirror to ourselves. ME sufferers who are experiencing incredible loss and rejection find it very difficult to hold on to any self-esteem.

ME throws up a real fear of the future because the future is so uncertain. The dark shadow of uncertainty hangs over all sufferers. Will I ever get better? What if I never get better? How much longer do I have to live like this? To live with this uncertainty on a daily basis can feel like a choking experience. Since there is no time-scale attached to the illness and therefore no end to look forward to, it is not surprising that I have heard sufferers describe their illness as 'a living death'. It has been said that some sufferers would rather have a terminal illness than have ME. They want to see an end to this 'living hell'. Many sufferers say that if only they knew the year of their release, or even a better patch of health, they could plan and so have something to look forward to. With so many hopes and dreams shattered, the road ahead can seem bleak and unending.

Coping with loss

I continue to be shocked by the scale of loss that ME sufferers experience. I believe that if others were aware of the enormity of the problem, they would be less quick to judge and condemn. I met a lady called Jane who had to give up her son because of her illness. The immense pain of this overwhelmed her as she struggled to tell me how she had collapsed at his eighth birthday party. After this, she had to come to terms with the fact that she was too ill to parent her child. She felt such a failure. She still wrestles with the guilt and pain of losing him, in spite of the fact that God intervened and worked a miracle in her life which enabled her to have him back. Jane tells her story in Chapter 11.

One sufferer told me that having ME is much worse than being registered blind. Karen has always been blind and so has learnt how to live with this disability and used to work, keep fit and lead a very active life. Now she can no longer work and has to live in a specially adapted flat because she needs a wheelchair to get around. Another sufferer thought he was dying before he was eventually diagnosed with ME, so, as a form of legacy, he wrote a series of poems for each of his three children, expressing his love for them. Understandably, many lose belief in a God who can allow the suffering of ME, and when religious beliefs are central to a person's identity this can cause great trauma.

Unexpected losses are particularly hard to come to terms with, partly because so many coping mechanisms that might have previously been an option are no longer available. In ME, people are confronted with the reality of themselves and their situation. As one friend said to me, 'If only I could have a holiday from myself.' For others it has become an opportunity to make life-changing discoveries because life no longer revolves around a treadmill of activity and 'doing'. As one sufferer comments, 'I'm working on the concept that "being" is more important than "doing". I can't *do* things for my family and with my family as I once could, but I can *be* for them in a way that is probably more important. I no longer feel that I have to prove anything to anyone by what I do, which is a surprisingly peaceful experience.'

Anger

Anger has been the most difficult emotion to deal with and probably the most damaging. I have raged at the unfairness of it all, feeling that I have been robbed of what I thought would be my golden years. I have been furious at the way I have been treated by doctors and enraged by the behaviour of people I thought were friends. I have been angry with my own body for letting me down.[3]

The problem with anger is that it can alienate us still further from people and so compound our loss. It is so hard to know what to do with the anger that wells up from within like an explosive force. I have struggled to find ways of expressing and releasing my anger and frustration and have taken it out on other people. This had a damaging effect on several close friendships for a while.

When one friend of mine prayed for me and prayed that God would give me peace, I found myself getting really angry and shouting out, 'I don't want peace, I want healing! I want healing for my knee and for this pain inside that's breaking my heart.' My friend was very taken aback, as I'm not known for my outbursts, but my words of anger echoed the frustration of six months of having to cope, of people not understanding, and the facade of pretending to be OK when I wasn't in order to protect everyone else's feelings. As I began to cry and release those feelings, my friend was able to gain some insight into my situation and could begin to empathize and draw alongside me. This incident proved to be a turning point in our friendship and has considerably aided further communication. I was being real with her and before God, and this is so often when real communication and transformation becomes possible.

But Why Me?

'The way I was . . .'

ME is said to affect certain personality types, frequently those who rush around trying to do too much. I was an achievement-orientated junkie. I had to keep 'doing' so that I could keep achieving. But the question is *why?* What we do in our spare time is a mirror to what is going on in the rest of our lives. If we can't balance our lives to include sufficient rest and relaxation, it may be worth asking the question *why?*

ME eventually became an investment for the rest of my life. I had to learn how to slow down. As the consultant said to me at the time, 'Only 1 per cent of the population gets away with pushing themselves to this degree, and why should you think that you are in that lucky 1 per cent?' I have never forgotten those words, and so ME became a training ground where I would be forced to learn how to pace myself. Coming to terms with the question *why?* is important because it is much easier to modify your lifestyle if you know what lies beneath the need to keep busy. Many sufferers readily admit that they still find it hard to strike a balance between activity and inactivity. Although ME is a severe teacher, this lesson is a hard one to learn. However, finding that point of balance is crucial.

You might find it helpful to consider some of the following questions:

Why did I need to be so busy? Should I have taken on less? Why did I allow my diary to become full in the first place? Why did I find it difficult taking time off? Is there some compulsive need that made me rush from place to place? Am I trying to keep some fear at bay? Did I rush around because I needed to be needed? Was my busyness hiding some gaping hole in my life?

Forgiveness Is Freedom

Forgiveness is something we all wrestle with. When we have a grievance against someone who has hurt us, it is natural to want to hold onto it so that we can make the other person suffer. The problem is that in not forgiving the other person, whether we feel our actions are justified or not, we actually damage ourselves more. The stranglehold of unforgiveness can further enmesh us and pull us down into the dark pit of bitterness, hate, resentment and despair. These negative emotions will further damage our health and can lead to depression.

It takes tremendous courage to face the pain and forgive all the people who have hurt you. ME sufferers unfortunately have a long list of grievances because of people's lack of understanding. The last thing sufferers feel like doing is forgiving, especially when they are already struggling to cope with the illness. Yet if 'forgiveness is freedom', sufferers cannot afford to be further imprisoned. One sufferer explains the nature of this struggle: 'I feel the misunderstanding and the comments you receive can be as damaging as the illness itself, and it's been a constant battle for me since I've been ill, forgiving people for their insensitivity or just lack of concern.'

Sometimes, I simply find it too hard to forgive, usually because some comment or hurtful remark continues to cut deeply into me. It is at these times that I have had to ask God to help me forgive. Forgiveness is a process, and I often need help with that process, especially when wounds are deeply rooted in the past. But the harder it is to forgive, the greater is the potential release for both you and the other person.

Forgiving God

Sometimes we have to learn how to forgive God as well as ourselves. Our grievance against God may be very real, though not necessarily rational. I blamed God for allowing my knee to be in such a state and for not protecting me from injury when I had specifically prayed for his protection while I was dancing in South Africa. My grievance was very real, but as I continued to argue with God over this issue, I realized that he did not tell me to leap off a wall: that was an impulsive action of mine and the cause of my injury. He probably had protected me from injury while I was dancing, and from catching malaria, another concern of mine. My flight was cancelled too, because the plane was discovered to be unsafe. Was this also his protection? However, God's protection did not extend to covering for my own stupidity, but then neither would most insurance policies! It was only as I began to stop arguing with God over this issue and let go of my grievance that I was able to forgive both God and myself. This then enabled me to begin to accept my situation and to ask God to help me.

The Value of Counselling

Counselling is not about giving advice and trying to sort out people's problems for them. Counsellors essentially support and encourage people so that they are better able to make their own choices. If you are able to say how you feel and explore your problems in a safe environment, with no fear of condemnation, you become more able to make informed choices about the issues affecting your life. The skills of counselling are essentially based on communication and empathetic listening.

In a society where people are becoming more isolated from their communities and from potential support structures, counselling has become increasingly important. As one counsellor explained, 'Many people just don't have a close friend that they can turn to in times of trouble, to pour their hearts out to, and so counsellors are fulfilling this role too.'

Clearly, close friendship is precious and the quality of sharing that can take place can be very beneficial, but there are times when certain issues may need to be addressed that require the specific expertise of a trained counsellor. It can become difficult to counsel a friend when the closeness of the relationship prevents objectivity, and if anything backfires as a result, the friendship may be at risk too.

When I had ME, the consultant immunologist suggested that I had counselling. At first, I resented the idea, because I thought this suggestion undermined the validity of my illness. However, I did agree that I needed help in coming to terms with the tremendous change that had suddenly swept through my life. In retrospect, I wish that I had sought help sooner, as counselling helped me adjust to the confines of the illness. Talking through feelings of anger and guilt is more constructive than suppressing emotions and letting them be driven inside, which can lead to depression.

Asking for help

Many sufferers have come to realize the important role counselling can play in helping them come to terms with ME and so manage it more effectively. The more they are able to express what is going on inside, the healthier will be their response to the illness. Asking for help is not a sign of weakness but a sign of courage. My biggest stumbling block in asking for help has been my pride. I don't like asking because I feel I should be able to cope. Am I admitting to failure if I seek help, and does that then damage my already fragile self-esteem? In my current situation it makes sense to ask for help from people who are skilled in counselling those coming to terms with illness, injury etc., and yet there's a part of me that feared asking, because I'm not terminally ill and I don't want others thinking I am making a fuss. Sometimes a fear of rejection can prevent us from asking. In the end I had to lay down my pride and admit I needed help and risk rejection or disappointment. These fears proved to be unfounded. The chaplaincy at the hospital where I sought help couldn't have been more understanding.

Counselling ME sufferers

I believe that it is important for counsellors to have some knowledge of ME if they are to be in a position to help and understand sufferers. A sufferer who is also a counsellor writes, 'Counselling needs to be client-centred, for many clients will feel they have not been adequately supported or listened to previously and that their words have been interpreted according to a preconceived theoretical stance.'[4]

The nature of the illness itself may cause problems for the counsellor if he or she does not take into account the effect that the illness has on the brain, causing emotional lability, loss of memory and word-muddles. The sufferer may look well but in reality be struggling to cope with the session, so it might be helpful if the session was shorter.

I found the counselling I received on a respite week particularly helpful. This was because the counsellor was part of an ME charity and so was more aware of the problems involved in counselling sufferers. We were also able to have the counselling in our rooms, which meant that I could lie down. This made a considerable difference, because sitting up is tiring and painful for ME sufferers. The flexibility of the appointment system meant that if we were feeling too ill, we did not have to break a fixed appointment, but could reschedule accordingly. Another advantage was that there was no energy expended on travelling to see the counsellor, which is an important factor when you are operating on minimal energy reserves.

What are the advantages of Christian counselling?

Christian counselling looks at the whole person. A Christian counsellor is trained to be aware of the physical, psychological and spiritual aspects and how they are intricately related and interwoven in each person. The Association of Christian Counselling defines Christian counselling as:

That activity which seeks to help people towards constructive change and growth in any or every aspect of their lives. The aim is to achieve this through a caring relationship and within agreed boundaries, according to Biblical truths, aims and methods, all practised within a framework of Christian commitment, insight and values.

I have benefited from Christian counselling because it has given me the opportunity to pour out my feelings about God in relation to my situation without fear of condemnation, knowing that the counsellor can identify with the struggle of being a Christian and will be able to offer prayer and support in this area too.

8

ALTERNATIVE APPROACHES TO ME

Natural Remedies

With no medical cure for ME, it is hardly surprising that most sufferers turn to the alternative health sector for help. Alternative medicine is becoming increasingly popular and sufferers may try many of the following treatments: acupuncture, reflexology, allergy testing, cytoxic testing, alternative allergy treatments, neutralisation therapy, aromatherapy, massage, candida treatment, dietary modification, dental amalgam removal, detoxification therapy, colonic irrigation, herbal medicines, evening primrose oil, magnesium, homeopathy, oxygen therapy, cognitive behaviour therapy, Alexander technique, probiotics, royal jelly, meditation and relaxation techniques and healing.

In 1992, a survey of six hundred sufferers indicated that, on average, they spent approximately £900 on alternative treatments and remedies, the most being £16,000.[1] Natural remedies, however, are not always harmless. Unfortunately, many sufferers have been exploited by those offering 'instant cures' or breakthrough treatments, so it is important to exercise caution.

There is no doubt that many sufferers benefit from alternative treatments and that these treatments can be helpful in reducing certain symptoms. They also doubtless benefit from being given more time and attention, being offered the kind of care and understanding that is so often lacking in conventional medicine. I will mention just a few here.

Massage

One sufferer writes:

> I was in such pain that every part of my body was sensitive to touch. I had a rash all over my skin, which I believe was a build-up of toxins. I was bloated particularly around my middle and under my arms and had terrible weakness in all my muscles. I couldn't even give my kids a hug: it was too painful. I was crying out to God, 'What can I do? I can't cope with this.' I then met a sufferer who had been helped through massage and so I decided to give it a try.
>
> My muscles had become so weak that the massage stimulated them to function. The masseuse was able to realign my knees, which tended to go out of joint, and kept them mobile. A lot of my symptoms eased. I did not have the energy to exercise but her massaging my muscles kept them from further deterioration. My whole body became less painful as she massaged the toxins away. I don't know how I would have kept going without this treatment.

EPD treatment

Many sufferers have food allergies and have found EPD (enzyme potentiated desensitization) treatment helpful as it offers gradually increasing relief from allergy symptoms. The treatment is a complex mixture of dilute extracts of common foods combined with an enzyme which activates the immune system's ability to respond to food dilutions.

Carol writes:

> I suffered with multiple allergies after a series of amalgam fillings. From that point onwards my immune system broke down and I struggled to walk. I was later diagnosed as having ME. The allergies continued to get worse until I became allergic to most foods. I became so completely allergic to the environment that I was unable to leave my room. My doctor had given me six months to live.
>
> My church fasted and prayed for a breakthrough for me, and as a result I found out about EPD treatment through Dr Dawes' book *Why ME?* I then got in touch with Dr Myhill, who agreed to treat me. I've had EPD treatment for several years and can now eat anything. Although I still have ME, there has been a dramatic improvement.

Many sufferers seem to benefit from a nutritional approach to ME. Information on a whole range of alternative treatments is available through Action for ME and the ME Association.

The Value of Meditation and Relaxation

In 1990, when I was ill, there was much talk about the benefits of transcendental meditation in the ME magazines. I felt unsure, however, about some of the ideas behind this form of meditation and so decided to explore Christian meditation. A sufferer later gave me a booklet explaining it:

Meditation is a mental and spiritual activity between an individual, or group, and God. The creation of a quiet space where one can be alone with God. The inner stillness in which God can speak, and an openness to God through which He can pour the gifts of His Spirit.

Meditation directs the mind away from self, and concentrates it upon God. It stops us thinking of ourselves, our difficulties, our needs, and lets the mind soar beyond all this to God. In the silence of meditation we are learning how to open our hearts to the healing power of God's love; then, because of the close link between our physical and mental states, the body responds in a variety of ways; it may be an increase in vitality, greater resistance to infection, the easing of tensions, pain or other physical disorders.[2]

Shortly after this, I remembered that my vicar's wife, Joyce Huggett, had just written a book about meditation and contemplative prayer and so I decided to buy *Open to God* in an attempt to have a go myself. It was through reading this book and trying to open myself to God through some of the relaxation techniques and meditations that I first began to hear God speak to me. I was amazed because I didn't feel that I really understood fully what I was doing, and so when I started hearing voices I thought I must be going mad. But as time went on, God continued to reveal to me that he would heal me. I had no idea that meditation and contemplation were such a powerful form of prayer. The deep relaxation and quality of rest that I experienced were incredible. Somehow, I had stumbled across a means to draw close to God's heart and so commune with the divine source of all healing. My journey into contemplative prayer and meditation had resulted in me being able to hear God, and this ultimately led to my recovery from ME. This form of prayer is still a very important part of my daily walk with God and is essential to my health and spiritual well-being. Consequently, I now lead sessions in relaxation, contemplation and meditation on ME retreats, so that others can experience the healing power of drawing close to God in this way. My relaxation and meditation CD *A Quiet Place* continues to help those sufferers who are not well enough to attend retreats (see Appendix 3).

One sufferer wrote:

> When I first heard *A Quiet Place*, I was in a ditch. I had been very ill, not a relapse, but relentless sinking from an already low point. I lay in bed with the curtains closed and decided to play your CD.
>
> The Lord blessed me immediately. I followed the relaxation method and it worked. Then I found it easy not only to visualize the picture you were creating but also to experience it. Through your words, God cleansed me of bitterness, physical and emotional, and replaced it with his golden love. The effect was peace and a strengthening of trust, a fortifying of my faith; in other words a lovely long cuddle! The result was a restoration of my ability to see beyond the grey blanket and to play a normal part in family life again.

The Value of Respite Care

One sufferer writes:

> I'm severely affected, bedbound/housebound, and need a lot of care. My wife has had to become my

full-time carer and so really needs a break, as we have three children too. I was hesitant about respite because my last experience, two years ago, was in a home full of active disabled people – wheelchair athletes some of them – and although the care was good, I was exhausted by the atmosphere. So this time, I decided to choose a large country house because it is a nursing home for old people.

I'm glad I followed my instincts. The quality of care was superb; I was encouraged to avoid using even one ounce of energy and was treated with dignity and compassion. No one gushed or embarrassed me, but when I was very ill with muscle cramps and nerve pain, or mental fog and loss of co-ordination, the help I needed was anticipated and provided.

But the most beneficial aspect of my stay was the friendship. The staff met me where I was and accepted me, and they reflected sunlight and brightened my greyness. I try to be so emotionally strong at home, not because I have to, but because there's so little left of my old macho life that I try to hang on to one last shred, I suppose. Here, I cried. It was a mixture of anger and happiness, mourning what I've lost and celebrating what I've gained, and lots of other things which needed to come out. It was a cleansing, a blessed relief which only occurred because I was in an environment where I was secure enough to allow myself to be weak, surrounded by professionals who became friends.

I benefited from the first residential ME respite course that Westcare ran in 1990. There were eight residential sufferers of varying ages attending the course, sharing accommodation in chalet-type cottages on a farm in Dorset. During the four days, there was a mixture of group talks, individual consultations with a doctor focusing on nutrition and managing ME, and the opportunity to talk to a counsellor. There were also several relaxation sessions. Shortly after the retreat I wrote:

> From a personal point of view, I found it a real pleasure just sharing each other's company and, as the week progressed, I began to feel that we had become more like a family and I was reluctant to leave. It was wonderful to experience such encouragement, support and kindness. I now feel confident that I have a much better idea of how to manage my illness in order to maximize my recovery. ME is reversible; there certainly is hope.

I still keep in touch with many sufferers from that weekend, as we developed a unique and special friendship through our mutual sharing in adversity.

Respite care was a turning point in my management of ME and helped to direct me along a path that led to my subsequent healing. Standing back from the illness so that you can see clearly where you are going is essential, but allowing God into the centre of ME and letting him direct your path is life-transforming.

It had been my vision for some time to offer retreats specifically for sufferers, so that I could share with others all that I had been privileged to receive. I have tried to incorporate these beneficial elements into the retreats, so that others whose lives are blighted by this terrible illness can experience hope and healing too. That vision was realized in Devon in 1996 when I led my first retreat for

ME sufferers. I have since led retreats in other parts of the country and have had the privilege of seeing three sufferers completely healed of ME. One severe sufferer literally got up out of her wheelchair and walked!

When I was visiting South Africa I had the opportunity to share this vision, as I believe that sufferers in other parts of the world can also really benefit from this approach. One South African sufferer wrote to me, 'Going on retreat seems like the most wonderful way to recharge, restore, refresh, renew etc., mentally, physically, spiritually and emotionally. It sounds like a dream!'

What is a Retreat?

Many people have found retreats to be a life-changing experience, and you don't have to be a monk or a mystic to go on one. Because life is being lived at such an unnatural pace, people are increasingly searching for a place to rest, recharge and find their own natural rhythm again. People are also searching for a spiritual dimension that will lead them into a place of inner peace and calm. Many people don't realize that Christianity offers this dimension. Jesus himself said, 'Come to me, all of you who are weary and carry heavy burdens, and I will give you rest' (Mt. 11:28, NLT).

The popular psalm 'The Lord is my shepherd' speaks of the rest, refreshment and restoration that God can bring to the depths of our being:

The LORD is my shepherd, I shall lack nothing.
He makes me lie down in green pastures,
he leads me beside quiet waters,
he restores my soul.

(Ps. 23:1–3)

Unfortunately, for some it is impossible to find the time to go on retreat, and yet time spent in this way is such an investment for health and productivity. Some may find going on retreat too threatening a concept, because they build their lives around busyness in order to avoid facing various issues. Illness, however, forces people to stop and to take stock. In a sense, ME was a cry from my body to stop. The whole of me was on overload as a result of overdrive. I certainly wouldn't have even considered a retreat before I was ill. I would have thought it a waste of time.

It is not surprising that the number of stress-related illnesses continues to grow, because we no longer know how and when to stop. I, like many others, have had to learn relaxation techniques, because I did not know how to relax. Even as a society, we have forgotten how to stop and listen to the needs of others, because we simply do not have time. Life was not meant to be lived at the pace we are living it and we are suffering the consequences. Unfortunately, all the labour-saving devices and gadgets have simply created even more time to work, rather than allowing us to relax and pursue other interests.

As I've been leading retreats, I've become aware of how desperate the need is for sufferers to experience healing in *all* areas of their personality, not just in their bodies. Many come, and it is as though the flame of their being is all but snuffed out. They have quite simply had enough. They are worn down spiritually, physically and emotionally. A retreat can provide the right environment not only for relaxation and refreshment, but also for deep restoration and healing. In an atmosphere of care and support, each sufferer is given permission to *be*, to *come as you are*, however you are feeling. To *let go* of the burden of illness and to find *shalom* – that deep peace and harmony within.

Often, retreat houses are set in spectacular grounds and countryside which adds to the sense of stillness, beauty and oneness with nature. I have led retreats at Buckfast Abbey in Devon, and the advantage of holding a retreat where there is a religious community resident is that you step into a stream of peace that has been created through continuous prayer. It is something I notice as soon as I arrive. I step into what I can only describe as a relaxing warm bath – a tangible peace, soaked in the presence of God. It's as though the clutter and junk that has accumulated in my life over the months is automatically shed as I walk through the door into this sanctuary. I can then let go of the emotional baggage that has accumulated and bask in the warmth of God's presence. Gradually, I begin to feel secure enough to open up from the depths of my being and find unconditional acceptance and love. In the dry barrenness of ME, these oases are essential. As one sufferer wrote, 'Just a note to let you know how much I enjoyed the retreat. God really touched me at a deep level. The meditation on God's love had a profound effect on me. I've always loved Jesus, but that weekend I fell in love with Him.'

How do sufferers benefit from retreats?

A real depth of friendship and befriending has emerged from each retreat. Sufferers no longer need to feel that they are on their own with ME; they are now in touch with a network of people. They benefit from the opportunity to share and be 'real' with each other in a supportive environment and so get to know each other very quickly. This depth of friendship has led to ongoing support and the setting up of various prayer groups. Many sufferers find the retreat to be a turning point in the management of their illness, because they have been able to step back from their situation possibly for the first time.

Here are some comments from those who have attended the ME retreats:

- *I came on the retreat to be spiritually uplifted and in hope of receiving more inner and physical healing. My prayer has been answered.*
- *I just had to write and thank you for leading last weekend. I found it a tremendously affirming and encouraging time. I have come away with a great joy in my heart, a new vision of hope. I see the great light and radiance of God ahead of me, but I'm not in such a hurry to get there!*
- *It has affirmed for me that the 'real me' with all the vitality and energy for life is still there. That person has not been lost for ever. Being in a retreat environment with fellow sufferers has been a liberating experience – we've had a lot of good laughs. It is almost as though a veil comes down between you and the 'well world': nobody's fault, it just happens. Here there is no veil – Praise the Lord!*
- *Although I didn't receive physical healing, God has ministered to me and dealt with a lot of guilt and feelings of inadequacy that I was carrying around. I have been blessed in so many ways.*
- *Liz's powerful testimony, her dance ministry, and the worship on Saturday night was wonderful. I really felt the presence of God in the room. I felt like skidding across the floor in my stockings –I wish I had now!*

The gift of silence

Silence is a gift that can refresh our whole being and bring us into the presence of God. Scripture tells us repeatedly to 'be still' and says that 'in quietness and in trusting confidence shall be your strength' (Is. 30:15, Amp). Silence is the language of lovers and it is through the intimacy of silence that we can draw closer to God. Silence also frees us to be ourselves and can awaken the deadness within us. It puts us in touch with both ourselves and our Creator. As Mother Teresa commented,

> We need silence to be alone with God, to speak to Him, to listen to Him, to ponder His words deep in our hearts. We need to be alone with God in silence to be renewed and to be transformed. Silence gives us a new outlook on life. In it we are filled with the energy of God Himself that makes us do all things with joy.
>
> God is a friend of the silence. His language is 'Be still, and know that I am God' (Psalm 46:10). He requires us to be silent to discover Him. In the silence of the heart God speaks.[3]

We don't have to go to a retreat centre to experience the gift of silence. One sufferer writes:

> Strangely, the relapse I am experiencing at the moment answers a need I have to spend time with God. It seemed as though the last few months have brought an explosion of ideas and thoughts, hopes and possibilities that have left me reeling somewhat, and I was beginning to feel homesick, I guess, for God. I wanted to go some place where I could spend quality time with Father without the distractions that were constantly springing up from normal surroundings ... not just domestic distractions but creative ones too. What I would have liked was to have gone to a quiet retreat house, in wonderful

wild countryside, to spend time in quiet contemplation and submission, listening to Father's voice in
the midst of his creation.

Details of a variety of retreats and retreat houses across
the country are listed in *Retreats* magazine, which can be
obtained through Christian bookshops. I have listed the
contact address for this magazine in Appendix 3 at the
back of the book. You can, of course, search the Internet to
find retreats and retreat centres locally and across the
world.

9

CAN GOD HELP ME?

Lifeline

The simple answer to this question is *yes*. I have spoken to countless sufferers and virtually all those who profess to have a faith describe how ME has strengthened their relationship with God and given them hope to go on. Most have experienced healing, whether it be physical, spiritual or inner healing. Many sufferers comment, 'I don't know how people cope with this illness without God.' Another sufferer admitted that she felt she would no longer be alive if it weren't for her faith. One couple who both have ME commented, 'Our relationship with God is the most important thing to us – it is our lifeline.'

My hope is that sufferers will discover the reality of this 'lifeline' for themselves, because I believe it is only God who can currently offer an authentic source of hope in this illness. The number of sufferers being healed of ME is significant, and yet somehow this information is suppressed. For many, though, God is the bitterest pill to swallow.

Only God has the power to break, transform and redeem what one sufferer describes as 'a curse from the pit of hell'.

I will exalt you, O LORD,
    for you lifted me out of the depths
    and did not let my enemies gloat over me.

> O LORD my God, I called to you for help
> and you healed me.
> O LORD, you brought me up from the grave;
> you spared me from going down into the pit.
> (Ps. 30:1–3)

God is a rescuer. His heart's desire is to set free those who are imprisoned. That help is as available to us now as it was to others many centuries ago.

Who is God?

'The only label that counts is love.' This is one of the most memorable and powerful statements I have ever heard in a sermon at my church. In a society that automatically categorizes, segregates and marginalizes, it is only love that crosses this divide and reaches out to unite. Essentially, *God is love.* The ultimate expression of this love, which will go to any lengths for us, is the death of

Jesus, his Son. God gave Jesus freely as this priceless gift for each of us, so that we might enjoy an intimate relationship with the Father and be free of anything that might separate us from him.

God's message to us can also be summed up in the word love, as Jesus said:

'Hear, O Israel, the Lord our God, the Lord is one. Love the Lord your God with all your heart and with all your soul and with all your mind and with all your strength.' ... 'Love your neighbour as yourself.' There is no commandment greater than these.

(Mk. 12:29–31)

God's promises to us

Christianity has its roots in Judaism, and in the Old Testament God revealed his character to Israel through seven covenant or promise-keeping names. These names are important because they demonstrate God's faithfulness and commitment to us today. He says:

- *I am with you*
- *I am your Peace*
- *I am the Good Shepherd*
- *I am your Provider*
- *I am your Banner (Victor)*
- *I am your Righteousness*
- *I am your Healer*

Furthermore, Jesus the Messiah, through his death and resurrection, became the new covenant and so fulfilled each of these covenant names. God does not change; it is only our opinion of him that changes. God says in the book of Exodus, 'I am the LORD, who heals you' (Ex. 15:26), and in the New Testament Jesus healed everyone

104

who came to him. Jesus' life and ministry are the most accurate reflection of the character of God: as he said, 'I and the Father are one' and 'I have come down from heaven not to do my will but to do the will of him who sent me' (Jn. 10:30; 6:38). God's promises provide all we need, and that abundance flows freely through knowing Jesus:

> As we know Jesus better, his divine power gives us *everything we need* for living a godly life. He has called us to receive his own glory and goodness! And by that same mighty power, *he has given us all his rich and wonderful promises.* He has promised that you will escape the decadence all around you caused by evil desires and that you will share in his divine nature.
>
> (2 Pet. 1:3–4, NLT, my emphasis)

God – the Father

In the parable of the Prodigal Son, we see the true nature of God's unconditional and all-embracing love. It is a

love full of compassion and mercy. *A love that runs to meet*. A love that doesn't require explanations or the fulfilment of certain conditions. His arms remain wide open for us and if we take just one step in his direction, he runs to meet us. Furthermore, his love is *a love that celebrates*. In the parable, nothing is too much trouble for the father; his love lavishes gifts on his son. The son is not required to crawl back on his hands and knees, which had always been my image of God's requirements.

Like the prodigal, I have known what it is like to return to the Father and be offered such a wonderful home-coming. In many ways life is a continual process of returning to God; our own humanness with all its conflicting desires can easily lead us away from God. But God has a heart for the lost. These are the very people he longs to rescue:

> I myself will tend my sheep and make them lie down, declares the Sovereign LORD. I will search for the lost and bring back the strays. I will bind up the injured and strengthen the weak.
>
> (Ezek. 34:15–16)

When my father died, I felt utterly bereft and fatherless. Being single seemed to further emphasize this loss. I had been close to him and he had always been my point of reference in life over everything. Some time later when I was praying I felt God draw especially close to me. I found myself overcome with tears and through those tears God reassured me that I was not fatherless, because he was my Father. I cannot begin to describe the precious-ness of that encounter. I have not felt the pain of my father's death as acutely since, because I now know that *God is my Father*.

Wrong concepts of God

Our image of God is often formed in childhood. When I first read the following account of 'Uncle George', written by a Jesuit priest, I knew that it accurately expressed my childhood image of God.

Uncle George lives in a formidable mansion, is bearded, gruff and threatening. We cannot share our parents' professed admiration for this jewel in the family. At the end of the visit, Uncle George turns to address us. 'Now listen, dear,' he begins, looking very severe, 'I want to see you here once a week, and if you fail to come, let me just show you what will happen to you.' He then leads us down to the mansion's basement. It is dark, becomes hotter and hotter as we descend, and we begin to hear unearthly screams. In the basement there are steel doors. Uncle George opens one. 'Now look in here, dear,' he says. We see a nightmare vision, an array of blazing furnaces with little demons in attendance, who hurl into the blaze those men, women and children who failed to visit Uncle George or to act in a way he approved. 'And if you don't visit me, dear, that is where you will most certainly go,' says Uncle George. He then takes us upstairs again to meet Mum and Dad. As we go home, tightly clutching Dad with one hand and Mum with the other, Mum leans over us and says, 'And now don't you love Uncle George with all your heart and soul, mind and strength?' And we, loathing the monster, say 'Yes I do,' because to say anything else would be to join the queue at the furnace.[1]

One sufferer comments that many Christians get caught up in a 'reward system', i.e. 'If I do things right, God will bless me more', or 'God has given me so much, I've got to repay him'. 'I believe God likes to give us good gifts anyway because he loves us so much.' I used to think that God had only healed me of ME so that I could help other sufferers. In other words, I had to pay God back for my healing. I didn't feel held to ransom over this, but it wasn't until a friend challenged me about it that I began to realize that God healed me because he loves me. My healing was an expression of that love and I don't have to pay him back. Knowing this has released me to help others more, because giving has now become a natural expression of the outpouring of God's love for me.

Is ME a punishment from God?

I used to describe ME as 'God's ultimate punishment'. But I now realize that God is not the overbearing Dickensian disciplinarian father figure I had once seen him as. He loves all that he created and does not sit in heaven deciding who to mete out suffering to next. To believe that God was punishing me for some past sin is to invalidate the centrality of the message of the cross, that Jesus 'was pierced for our transgressions' and that he 'took up our infirmities and carried our diseases', as spoken through the prophet Isaiah:

> Surely he took up our infirmities
>   and carried our sorrows,
> yet we considered him stricken by God,
>   smitten by him, and afflicted.
> But he was pierced for our transgressions,
>   he was crushed for our iniquities;
> the punishment that brought us peace was upon him,
>   and by his wounds we *are healed*.
>   (Is. 53:4–5, my emphasis)

In considering whether to blame God for our illness, I believe we need to look at our lifestyle before we developed ME. Clearly, in some cases there may not be obvious contributing factors. However, I can see why I developed ME and so never felt the question 'Why me?' was appropriate. I had been burning the candle at both ends, and was relentlessly pushing myself. I was struggling with stressful life events, and was not feeding myself properly or giving my body time to rest and recover. One sufferer writes, 'I don't believe in a God who wants people to be sick. Though in my own case, I have to admit and accept that I did not take enough care of myself before or after becoming ill. Basically I'd gone through life doing my own thing, very much with the accent on "doing".'

Many sufferers fall into this category, and with hindsight realize that they have pushed themselves too hard. Is that God's fault? No, I don't believe it is, though he makes a good scapegoat! As I mentioned before, when I was ill the consultant immunologist said to me, 'Only 1 per cent of the population gets away with pushing themselves like you have done. Why should you think that you are in that lucky 1 per cent?' He was right. I was suffering the consequences of overstressing my body and so really there was no one to blame but myself.

Why suffering?

People often say, 'How could a God of love allow such a thing to happen?' I don't know the answer to this question. Suffering is a mystery. But God is able to transform our suffering as well as use it to help others. As one sufferer writes: 'There are some who readily offer up their souls to God and yet withhold their bodies from his accepting trust. However limited we may feel ourselves to be, once we offer up the agony of our own particular disability we can move into freedom and fulfilment.'

I have struggled to understand how God can allow someone to have ME as well as another illness or disability. When a woman who is both blind and a severe ME sufferer first contacted me, I remember being really angry with God and saying to him, 'Isn't being blind enough?' I have since met sufferers who also have cancer. A profoundly deaf young sufferer writes, 'In one way, ME saved me from myself. I was looking for an opportunity to rebel and I thought university might give me the opportunity to do so. Having ME stopped that and ensured that my relationship with God continued. However, it's hard when you know that God has the power to save you from suffering but hasn't.'

Another sufferer who has chronic scoliosis writes, 'Whereas the disability, pain and deformity were beginning to become central to my living, I now understand that being what God has made me is central to my living and the rest is incidental.'

I remember feeling as though I was 'in prison' again when I first injured my knee, and was very distressed. However, one sufferer wrote to me, saying, 'You are not in prison; that is just a state of mind.' Another sufferer comments, 'It is not suffering that is the problem, because none of us are exempt from it, but what we do with it. There are some people who climb into themselves and then suffering becomes a prison.'

When God created each of us, he created a masterpiece in his own image. He created us to be free and healthy. I think that it must be painful for God to witness the extent of people's suffering and to see that image marred. How angry he must be at the injustice of ME, to see his children suffer so. God cares passionately about each of us and

110

wants to help. No father could bear to stand by help-lessly, watching his child suffer.

In Search of the Truth

In my early twenties I began to say, 'There has to be more to life than this.' It wasn't that my life was awful, it just seemed as though somehow there had to be something more. At the time I didn't realize that I was expressing a deep longing for a spiritual dimension, for that ultimate completeness in God. I seemed to have everything; a good job with prospects, a new car, my own house, and yet there was something missing. I visited an ex-teacher of mine who is a Christian and saw how her family had such a joy even though they lived very simply, with few material possessions. This intrigued me, as I had thought that it was material possessions and a good job that brought happiness. Now I had all this, I was still not satisfied.

Each of us has a thirst for a spiritual dimension because we were created as triune beings: body, soul and spirit. Many people, like myself, who have had bad experiences of the church do not see God as the natural way to fill this 'hole', and so it is not surprising that the occult has become so popular. People quite naturally equate God with 'the church', which often seems so outdated, dull and boring, and so assume that God has nothing to offer them. This could not be further from the truth, as I was eventually to discover.

However, at a time in my early twenties when I desperately needed help, I didn't even consider that turning to God was an option. He wasn't the God of love that I have since discovered, but the God of fear, condemnation and divine retribution, a sadistic tyrant

111

who sought vengeance. Who would want to turn to such a God for help? Consequently, I became interested in the occult. But this didn't seem to have the answers I was seeking either, and resulted in me feeling more desperate. After many years, triggered by the trauma of my father's terminal illness, I began my own search for God. Later, in ME, I was to experience the life-changing reality of those early faltering steps, as I discovered the tangible reality of God's presence, which for me was undeniable proof that he existed.

Many sufferers have been hurt through the church and have experienced rejection and even, in some cases, persecution. When I have prayed with sufferers about these issues and repented on behalf of the church, this has released the person into a place where they can let go of the pain and begin to forgive. So often these bad experiences are a blockage to finding God. Many of us carry a lot of unhelpful religious baggage from the past and so may need to ask God for a fresh revelation of himself. Only then will we be able to meet God in a new way, free from the pain of those experiences.

Christianity is not about a set of oppressive rules; it is a personal journey of discovery. We cannot follow someone else's path. It is a journey that we need to be free to choose ourselves, without pressure from others. Indoctrination did not lead me to God; it turned me away from him. A real relationship with God is not about attending church regularly; it's about searching for the truth and reality of God. As one sufferer comments, 'I'd been christened and confirmed, so on paper I was a believer. In reality I had gone through the rituals and then left when I was a teenager, disillusioned with religion that did not seem to offer anything apart from ritual.'

ME has proved to be a pathway to God for so many sufferers. My own journey through ME brought me face to face with the reality of God. It felt like the ultimate challenge – did God exist or didn't he? I'd got to the point in my illness where there seemed so little quality of life left that I didn't want to live any more. Sheer desperation led me to God. I had nothing left to lose. It was in this place of total surrender and submission to God that I experienced his presence. God met me and I met God. As in the parable of the Prodigal Son, I didn't have to crawl my way back to the Father, grovelling on my hands and knees: as I let go, he rushed to meet me. How long, I wonder, had he been waiting for that very opportunity to help me?

Who Am I in God?

I once heard a counsellor use the expression, 'Blessed are those who are content with themselves', and it really made me think about my own level of self-acceptance. Our self-acceptance is often a measure of the freedom we experience both to love and to be loved by others and to be at peace. Many of us struggle with low self-esteem and this is further compounded by a long-term illness or disability. As one sufferer comments,

It is a sad truth that some people find it hard to accept themselves and therefore experience difficulty in believing God's acceptance. Acceptance is life-giving and necessary, and God constantly proves his acceptance of us if we let him. But when we are able to take our eyes off ourselves long enough to seek him, then we will surely find acceptance.

One of the most helpful things I have done recently is to look at who I am in God. It has revolutionized how I see myself, because however worthless I may feel at times, I know that God does not see me in this way and it is his opinion that counts, not other people's. Knowing our place in God is vital because it gives us stability. You may want to develop your own list using a concordance and Bible, or you may find my list helpful.

1. I am chosen

For he chose us in him before the creation of the world to be holy and blameless in his sight. In love he predestined us to be adopted as his sons through Jesus Christ, in accordance with his pleasure and will – to the praise of his glorious grace, which he has freely given us in the One he loves.

(Eph. 1:4–6)

2. I am loved

I have loved you ... with an everlasting love. With unfailing love I have drawn you to myself.

(Jer. 31:3, NLT)

[Christ] loved me and gave himself for me.

(Gal. 2:20)

As the Father has loved me, so have I loved you.

(Jn. 15:9)

And I pray that you, being rooted and established in love, may have power, together with all the saints, to grasp how wide and long and high and deep is the love of Christ.

(Eph. 3:17–18)

114

3. *I belong to God*

Fear not, for I have redeemed you;
  I have called you by name; you are mine.

(Is. 43:1)

…your life is now hidden with Christ in God.

(Col. 3:3)

4. *I am fearfully and wonderfully made*

For you created my inmost being;
  you knit me together in my mother's womb.
I praise you because I am fearfully and wonderfully
    made…
My frame was not hidden from you
  when I was made in the secret place.
When I was woven together in the depths of the
    earth,
  your eyes saw my unformed body.
All the days ordained for me
  were written in your book
  before one of them came to be.

(Ps. 139:13–16)

5. *I am a child of God*

How great is the love the Father has lavished on us,
that we should be called children of God!

(1 Jn. 3:1)

6. *I am precious to God*

Since you are precious and honoured in my sight,
  and because I love you,
I will give men in exchange for you,
  and people in exchange for your life.

(Is. 43:4)

115

7. *I am free from condemnation*

Therefore, there is now no condemnation for those who are in Christ Jesus.

(Rom. 8:1)

8. *I am a new creation*

Therefore, if anyone is in Christ, he is a new creation; the old has gone, the new has come!

(2 Cor. 5:17)

9. *I am God's masterpiece*

For we are God's masterpiece. He has created us anew in Christ Jesus, so that we can do the good things he planned for us long ago.

(Eph. 2:10, NLT)

10. *I am forgiven*

For I will forgive their wickedness
and will remember their sins no more.

(Jer. 31:34)

11. *I am strong in God*

I have learned the secret of being content in any and every situation, whether well fed or hungry, whether living in plenty or in want. I can do everything through him who gives me strength.

(Phil. 4:12–13)

12. *I am a delight to God*

He will take great delight in you,
he will quiet you with his love,
he will rejoice over you with singing.

(Zeph. 3:17)

13. I am fathered by God

...A father to the fatherless...

(Ps. 68:5)

For you did not receive a spirit that makes you a slave again to fear, but you received the Spirit of sonship. And by him we cry, '*Abba*, Father'.

(Rom. 8:15)

14. I am God's beloved

'In that coming day,' says the LORD, 'you will call me "my husband" instead of "my master"'.

(Hos. 2:16, NLT)

15. I will never be forgotten or abandoned by God

...God has said, 'Never will I leave you;
    never will I forsake you'.

(Heb. 13:5)

Can a mother forget the baby at her breast
    and have no compassion on the child she has
    borne?
Though she may forget,
    I will not forget you!
See, I have engraved you on the palms of my hands.

(Is. 49:15–16)

The Desert of Illness

The poem 'Footprints' is a reminder that God will always walk with us, whatever we go through, and when we feel we can't even stand, let alone take another step, he will carry us. This is a wonderful picture of God, the Father, looking after his children. It reminds me of those special times as a child, when my little feet could walk no further and my father would lift me high onto his broad shoulders.

FOOTPRINTS

One night
I dreamed a dream. l was
walking along the beach
with my Lord. Across the dark
sky flashed scenes from my life.
For each scene, I noticed two sets
of footprints in the sand, one
belonging to me and one to my Lord.
When the last scene of my life shot
before me I looked back at the foot-
prints in the sand and to my sur-
prise, I noticed that many times
along the path of my life there was
only one set of footprints. I realized
that this was at the lowest and sad-
dest times of my life. This always
bothered me and I questioned
the Lord about my dilemma.
'Lord, you told me when I
decided to follow You, You
would walk and talk with
me all the way. But I'm
aware that during the
most troublesome times
of my life there is only
one set of footprints. I
just don't understand
why, when I needed You
most, You leave me.' He
whispered, 'My precious
child, I love you and will
never leave you never, ever,
during your trials and test-
ings. When you saw only
one set of footprints it
was then that I
carried you.'[2]

118

Our feelings are very unreliable, particularly in times of illness and difficulty. A friend of mine cried out to God in despair, 'Where are you, God? I can bear anything but you withdrawing your presence from me.' After many months of struggling to find God, she realized that God hadn't deserted her, but in fact was so close that he was out of focus.

God cares about the desert we are stranded in and longs to shelter and protect us:

In a desert land he found him,
    in a barren and howling waste.
He shielded him and cared for him;
    he guarded him as the apple of his eye ...

(Deut. 32:10)

Whatever we are going through, and even though we might not be able to feel his presence, God promises to be with us and says, 'Never will I leave you; never will I forsake you' (Heb. 13:5). In the Gospel of Matthew, Jesus says, 'I will be with you always, to the very end of the age' (Mt. 28:20).

One sufferer had this revelation about her illness during an ME retreat. She writes:

During the meditation this morning, I felt that God gave me a picture of a huge boulder. On the boulder were chains. I was attached to the chains. To my left I sensed the presence of Jesus and the chains were attached to him as well. Other sufferers were present, and the boulder was drawing us very slowly through the desert. All the time the boulder was preceding us. This picture is contrary to how I have envisaged ME before. I've always considered it as a huge dark shadow, a hideous burden, never as something leading the way! I was reminded of the scripture: *'Because of your great compassion you did not abandon them in the desert. By day the pillar of cloud did not cease to guide them on their path, nor the pillar of fire by night to shine on the way they were to take'.*

(Neh. 9:19)

This picture is a wonderful confirmation of the way God can transform our circumstances and turn them around so that the very thing that has imprisoned us can be used to release us. God is able to transform anything that we are prepared to give him.

10

THE RESURRECTION OF
HOPE –JESUS

A New Start

*I am the way and the truth and the life. No-one comes to
the Father except through me.*

(Jn. 14:6)

From the beginning of creation man rebelled against God
because he thought he knew better. This rebellion
brought sin and sickness into what was a perfect world.
That legacy continues today, but because of his love for us
God found a way to redeem his beloved creation through
Jesus. God allowed his Son to endure the alienation and
separation of the cross. Jesus' death on our behalf is a
message from God for each of us that says, 'I love you
that much.' It is only through this precious gift that we
can experience healing and can have access to 'life in all
its fullness'. It is through the cross that we can receive
forgiveness, a forgiveness that offers us a fresh start, a
new beginning – the slate is wiped clean. This concept of
forgiveness is foundational to Christianity. Forgiveness
cannot be earned: it is a gift. The death and resurrection
of Jesus offers healing that will embrace every part of our
being so that we can experience wholeness. It sets us free
to look forward to the future with hope, as Deni Newman
expresses in this poem:

JESUS

I was in a high place
and could see far and wide
broken homes, broken hearts, broken people.
I was suffering in agony,
but for them I cried
and their brokenness held me crucified.
No one could share
that burden of sorrow
as my heart also broke
and I died.

I was dead, but my dying had
broken the chains –
broken sin, broken illness, broken death;
For my name is JESUS, Name above names,
the one who lives! The one who reigns!
And I share
your burden of sorrow
for my heart also broke
when you cried.
I'm alive! And my living has
broken the lie –
broken fear, broken darkness, broken pride.
I shall speak to the broken ones when they cry,
I shall fill them until they are satisfied.
In me they can share
the joy of new life
for their healing came
when I died.

Jesus Walks With Us

Jesus was both human and God, and so endured all the problems and vulnerabilities of the human condition, except sin, as well as the opposition to being godly. The scriptures speak repeatedly of how Jesus was moved with compassion for those suffering. When Jesus saw Mary weeping because her brother Lazarus had died, he

'was deeply moved in spirit and troubled', and then wept. Even when Jesus came to the tomb where his friend Lazarus lay, he was 'once more deeply moved', yet he knew that he would raise Lazarus from the dead (Jn. 11:17–44).

123

Whatever we suffer, only Jesus has the right to say, 'I know how you feel.' He is the only person who can fully identify with our pain and walk with us in it. I once heard someone say that 'Jesus walks at the speed of love'. His timing is perfect. The incident on the road to Emmaus is a beautiful picture of Jesus walking with us. After the death of Jesus, the disciples are grief-stricken. Two of them wander down the road to Emmaus utterly desperate, feeling that everything is lost and that all hope is gone. To make matters worse, Jesus' body has been stolen too. 'As they talked and discussed these things with each other, Jesus himself came up and walked along with them; but they were kept from recognising him' (Lk. 24:15–16).

Jesus walked alongside them at their pace, allowing them to unburden their grief without judgement. He listened as they expressed their disappointment and sense of hopelessness ('We had hoped...). He then reassured them by explaining 'what was said in all the Scriptures concerning himself' (Lk. 24:27). But it was not until Jesus broke bread with them that 'their eyes were opened and they recognized him' (Lk. 24:31). Within an hour, the two friends were able to turn back to Jerusalem and join the rest of the disciples. Jesus always walks with us, whether we recognize him or not.

Does God Heal Today?

Healing is a controversial subject, even in the church. In the healing of the paralysed man in the Gospel of Mark (Mk. 2:1–12), it was the religious people who objected to what Jesus was doing. The issue, in this case, was not so much the healing as the blasphemy of Jesus saying, 'Son, your sins are forgiven.' This incident represents one of the many arguments in which Jesus became entwined, yet he continued to heal then and still heals today, despite the controversy.

I heard an interesting sermon on this subject by the Principal of an Anglican theological college. He said that thirty years ago he would have said that healing only happened in Jesus' time, not today, and that this view reflected that of the churches at the time. He commented, 'But God does heal today through the ministry of the Holy Spirit. We live in an age of the Spirit, and before, the church was reading the New Testament through ridiculous spectacles. I have seen people healed emotionally, spiritually and physically.'

Reading the gospels, it is perfectly clear that Jesus healed all those who came across his path and that this was not dependent on the person fulfilling certain criteria first:

> And whatever their illness and pain, or if they were possessed by demons, or were epileptics, or were paralysed – he healed them all.
>
> (Mt. 4:24, NLT)

While I have been writing this book, God has challenged me over my views about healing. I have had to expand them to accommodate a God who is much larger than any box I may care to put him in. Where I have felt dubious about certain healing ministries, God has challenged me. Time and time again, God will take us back to our point of prejudice so that we expand our thinking. He is not a slot-machine God, but the God of surprises. Consequently, it is impossible to lay down rigid rules for healing, because God is greater that any theory. Perhaps if there were a formula, people would be tempted to follow it just to gain their healing and then dump the Healer!

Being miraculously healed of ME does not make me an expert on healing. Many sufferers have wanted to know my 'secret' so that they can follow it and become healed. But the only formula that never changes is God, and the greatest healing has to be in our relationship with him. We were created for intimacy with God and it is a relationship of completeness and wholeness that is eternal, and so will last long beyond our physical bodies. It is only out of this relationship that the healing flows.

There is no doubt in my mind that God wants to heal us: as he says in Jeremiah 30:17, 'I will restore you to health and heal your wounds.' He also tells us in Hebrews and Isaiah that by his wounds we *are* healed; in other words that healing is available to us now. The difficulty is that we see only a fragment of what is a much bigger picture – God's unique plan for each of our lives. Healing is a process. This is an unpopular message to a culture that expects instant answers to problems. God can and does heal instantly, but in searching for the 'quick fix' we can miss out on the fullness of what God wants to do in each of us. God cares about our whole being and wants to heal us emotionally, spiritually and physically. He is a truly 'holistic' God and physical healing may not be his first priority.

A parent is not purely concerned with the physical well-being of their child, but with their overall growth, development and stability. God, our Father, cares about our total health and well-being and longs to restore every part of us, but this is only possible through our relationship with him. When I injured my knee, it was as though every part of me was thrown out of alignment, not just my kneecap. God has been slowly healing me, but 'from the inside out'. And that healing began with the restoration of my relationship with him – the source of all healing.

God wants to meet us at the point of our deepest need, and to touch the root of our problem. At the end of one retreat, a sufferer summed up the weekend by spontaneously singing about how God had touched her from the 'inside out'. God does not force his way in: we have to allow him access to the depths of our being, and it is here that 'whole person' transformation becomes possible. Jennifer Rees Larcombe, a well-known Christian writer and speaker who had ME, has spoken about the inner peace and healing she received, which she called 'peace-joy'. This 'peace-joy' was a real gift from God and enabled her to live with her severe disabilities. She wrote about her experience in *Beyond Healing*. Some years later, she was healed physically too, and wrote the book *Unexpected Healing*.[1]

God does heal people through well-known healing ministries and meetings, but he is equally able to heal us at home though our local communities and churches. There is no limit to the way God can operate. I don't believe that sufferers are meant to put their lives 'on hold', waiting for a miracle to happen; nor are they meant to live from one healing experience to another. God invites us to continually bathe in the river of his healing presence, in the 'stream of healing' where the miraculous is still a possibility.

It concerns me that some sufferers who have experienced sudden dramatic physical healing have then somehow lost their healing. Many have a tendency to take their healing and 'run with it', often rushing around in overdrive. As I have already said, ME is a severe teacher and there are many lessons to be learned both within the illness and beyond it. We need to learn how to walk in time with our Shepherd, the Divine Physician, every step of the way. Psalm 139 in the Living Bible says, 'You chart the path ahead of me, and tell me where to stop and rest.' Many busy Christians, as in the story of Mary and Martha (Lk. 10:38–42), are also having to learn that God is more concerned about our 'being' than our 'doing', even if our 'doing' is for him.

'Mustard seed' faith

Unfortunately, many people have been told that they have not been healed because they do not have enough faith. Consequently sufferers have felt condemned by this. But the Bible tells us that we only need faith the size of a mustard seed, which is tiny.

Some sufferers, however, may not even have a mustard seed of faith when it comes to healing. I doubted whether God could heal my knee. Because I'd already been physically healed once by God, I've found myself wondering whether God could heal me again. Did he want to? Was he able to? Had I already received my portion of physical healing for this life? Was it right to ask again? These were some of my doubts and questions.

There are also many people who have a lack of revelation concerning Jesus as Healer, and this can be the greatest hindrance to our healing. I have found it vitally important to spend time looking at all the Scriptures on healing in the gospels to reinforce my faith, so that I can pray for healing. As a result, I have concluded that there is no reason why God shouldn't or couldn't heal my knee, whether it be through an operation or naturally. If God loves me, he wants the best for me, so I have to trust in his abundant provision as I plant that tiny seed of faith in a big God.

Do you want to become well?

Although many people can virtuously list all the benefits

of suffering, this can sometimes act as a block. One chronic sufferer I spoke to was clearly struggling with the concept of healing, because it represented too much of a threat to him. He had got used to his restricted lifestyle and feared change. This was causing a blockage that prevented him being able to ask God for healing, yet he freely admitted that he knew God could heal him. When someone challenged me over my knee and asked me if I wanted to be healed, I was annoyed. I thought this was a ridiculous question, but I was alarmed at my inability to respond. My knee had caused me no end of pain and difficulty and here I was hesitating to say 'yes'. It was helpful to be challenged in this way, so it is not surprising that Jesus asked a blind beggar the question, 'What do you want me to do for you?' (Lk. 18:41).

As one sufferer commented, 'The temptation when you are chronically ill is to sit around analysing and rationalising everything.' God wants us to be specific in our prayers and to share with him the desires of our heart. We are meant to be actively involved in our healing. He tells us to 'Keep on asking, and you will be given what you ask for' (Mt. 7:7, NLT). A well-known evangelist once said, 'God's delays are not his denials.' We are told in Scripture that God always answers our prayers; the problem is that he doesn't always answer them when or in the way we would like.

To help me pray for healing I have found it helpful to ask myself a series of questions:

- *What do you want?*
- *What are you holding on to?*
- *Do you believe God can heal you?*
- *Do you want to be healed?*
- *Do you believe God wants to heal you?*
- *Do you believe God will heal you?*

When I have got stuck on one particular question, it has really helped me to highlight what is going on in my thought processes and to ask God to help me overcome this hurdle. However, asking too many questions and trying to analyse God can create barriers too.

11

TESTIMONIES OF HEALING AND MUCH, MUCH MORE ...

Prayer continues to offer a higher success rate in terms of recovery from ME than any medical treatment. I could easily write a separate book detailing testimonies of people I've met who have been healed of ME, there are so many. In this chapter, however, I have chosen to highlight just a few.

In the healing of the paralysed man in Mark 2 it is not the man's faith that heals him, but that of his friends. God heals people of great faith and those of no faith whatsoever. Jane, who gives her testimony below, didn't even know God and yet received healing.

Jane's Testimony

I came down with ME in 1993. As far as I was concerned it was just a bad dose of flu at first. I should have rested, and I spent months and months regretting that I hadn't. Day by day I seemed to manage less. One day I would go as far as the local shopping centre and then be exhausted once home. Then I could just about manage the local shop and then the corner of the road before I was overcome with exhaustion.

I shall never forget what happened next. It was my son's birthday party. I remember slicing the birthday cake and feeling extremely ill, and then I collapsed. I was scared and I knew my son was too. We waited for the ambulance to arrive. Over the next few weeks I discovered how ill-equipped doctors and medical staff were to deal with ME. My son went to stay in France for the summer and I was being looked after by relatives. I remember that summer as being one of extremes, alternating between despair and optimism, collapse and reasonable mobility. It was soon obvious that I was too ill to have my son with me and that he would have to stay in France with my ex-husband. The university also told me that I would lose my job if I didn't return to work in the next six months. With this added stress I was going downhill fast. My whole world seemed to be crashing down on me.

Several months later I totally relapsed and became bedridden. I now needed more help. All my meals were prepared for me and I was given help having a bath and washing my hair. I usually didn't see anyone for 24 hours at a time until the care assistant arrived the following day. The sense of loss was overwhelming. The mixture of grief, guilt and anger was very hard to bear. For the first time in my life I felt like I had no control over anything.

Having tried various alternative treatments and getting nowhere, I then turned to what seemed to be the only option left – healing. Around this time, I came across an article written by a man who said he'd been healed of ME during a service at a church called Peniel, in Essex. I also heard about two people from my local group who'd received healing and they were both severe sufferers. The following day, I rang the church to make arrangements. I was desperate, and open to anything if it meant getting rid of this prison I was in. I was convinced that if only I were well, life would be perfect. (Life, of course, hadn't been perfect before I became ill, but it certainly looked that way from a sick bed!) I'd lost my health, my son, my job, my independence, my financial security, my social life.

I was wheeled into the church and given a lounger at the front. During the service, the speaker came over to me and prayed for me. I did not feel anything, no heat, no tingling, nothing, but I knew I was different.

That night I had no sleep. Yet the following day, apart from a few rests, I stayed up, made myself my first cup of tea in over nine months and gave myself a bath for the first time in over nine months too. It sounds very little to a healthy person, but for me it was a miracle! Life was good. Although the symptoms were still present, they were much reduced... It was time to go back home.

The fact that I wasn't completely cured was a mystery to me. If God healed, then surely it would be complete. Why is it some devoted Christians are not healed and yet I wasn't a Christian and I received healing? I also realize how easy it is for someone who has made such an improvement to become rather smug about it, and find reasons for the lack of healing in others.

My son returned to live with me in the summer of 1996. He was now 12 years old. We had lost three precious years together. I still have problems coming to terms with that separation and find it difficult to talk about. However, I made it to the airport to collect my son. What an experience. Actually seeing me there was a shock for him, but he guessed by the tone and strength of my voice that something had happened.

The fact that I was no longer bedridden after so long was not just the power of positive thinking. I'm not convinced that positive thinking can make such a difference overnight! I'd started by looking for physical healing and found so much more, and although my healing is not complete I have no reason to doubt that with God's help it will be done one day. When I think back to how ill I used to be and life without my son... I don't ever want to take life for granted again!

When I first met Jane and she told me her story, I was moved to tears. God, the loving Father, had met this mother at her point of need and healed her sufficiently to have her son back. God had given Jane her heart's desire, even though she didn't know him. What an amazing testimony! Jane has since become a Christian.

Claire's Testimony

Claire developed ME the same year as me, 1989, and was also healed in 1991. When we first bumped into each other in 1996 we realized how much we had in common.

I'd been burning the candle at both ends for some time. I was working four days a week, running around after two young children and helping to gut our cottage. I had a series of infections, which I was given antibiotics for, and I believe these weakened my immune system. I then got flu and never seemed to recover.

134

I was in severe pain. Every part of my body was sensitive and I couldn't even give the kids a hug, it was too painful. I was totally bedridden for the first five weeks and after that still needed to spend days in bed. I struggled with severe lethargy, tiredness, loss of memory and confusion. I felt robbed of my life and frustrated that I couldn't even look after my family.

I had a determination to try anything I could to get better, and did. A change of diet helped, as I also had Candida albicans. Massage seemed to reduce the toxins and stimulated my immune system. But the only thing that kept me going was my faith and trust in God and knowing that when I was weak I could call on his strength. I cried out to God, 'What can I do? I can't cope with this.'

I was encouraged by a friend to go to a Christian meeting. I did not want to go because I didn't feel well enough to cope with it. Some people there told me about the healing that had happened the previous week, but I was really sceptical. However, when it was time to receive prayer for healing, I found myself getting up, even though I could hardly stand because of the ME.

As I was prayed for, what felt like a bolt of lightning seemed to go through me from the top of my head to the tips of my toes. A real warmth and light flooded through and I found myself on my knees sobbing. The stress and anxiety lifted and I was able to think clearly for the first time in eighteen months. I knew something wonderful had happened – God had touched me.

The first thing I wanted to do, now my head was clear, was to read my Bible. I found myself turning to Proverbs 4:20–22:

> My son, pay attention to what I say;
>   listen closely to my words.
> Do not let them out of your sight,
>   keep them within your heart;
> for they are life to those who find them
>   and health to a man's whole body.

As I studied this passage over the coming months, these scriptures became a reality in my life. My body became stronger and within six months I was able to walk six miles. It is thirteen years ago now that God healed me and I'm still well.

Shortly after Claire was healed of ME her husband became a Christian. He could not deny the huge change in Claire that he was witnessing, and knew that it could be nothing else but God, because they had tried virtually everything else.

Richard's Testimony

I met Richard in 1997 at a messianic conference where he gave his amazing testimony. Richard was an orphan and had recently discovered that he is Jewish. He has written a book called *A Loving Father*[1] which speaks of Richard's love for his children – a love that will go to any lengths to get his children back, even prison. Richard believes that God's love is like this.

'I don't know what it is,' said the doctor, 'probably just a type of flu virus.'
  As the winter went on and my illness didn't improve, I once again felt my chances of competing in the Olympics slipping away. It was to be bye-bye Montreal Olympics.

I needed a rest. I'd been working eighteen-hour days for the last five years. There were times when I felt quite well, then boom, my world would crash around me as I collapsed, and everything went haywire again. I never had any energy and my strength was deteriorating rapidly. The next three or four years saw the constant fluctuation of my health while money ran out. Our standard of living had dropped drastically and it must have been very hard for my wife to have a semi-crippled man around the house instead of a super-fit athlete.

I figured I was bullet proof and never thought of being ill, except for an occasional asthma attack. Boy, was I wrong. Many days now I couldn't get out of a chair or do the simplest household chore. I couldn't even lift my little Jean off the floor; she only weighed about 12lb. The shot put that I had thrown for twenty years weighed more than she did, and with my dead lift weight training exercises I had been lifting 600 or 700lb from the floor. So this was soon to show me the disastrous effects that the ME was having on my body.

Richard's three children were taken away from him to another country. His determination to get them back led him to desperate measures. Unfortunately this resulted in a prison sentence. So Richard, a severe ME sufferer and chronic asthmatic, was not only imprisoned by the illness, but behind bars too! While in prison, Richard received an unexpected visit from an evangelist.

'There's an evangelist by the name of Barry Kissel here to see you,' the prison vicar said. 'He feels the Lord wants him to visit someone in prison. Would you be interested in meeting him?' he said.

'Sure would, the name's familiar,' I said.

'Should be, you're reading his book,' said Bill.

'Do you mind if I pray for you,' Barry said.

'I would like that very much, I need all the help I can get.'

As Barry started to pray for the Lord to heal my ME and asthma, I felt this incredible heat pass through Barry's hands into my chest. It was as if my whole upper body was on fire. Barry carried on praying and I knew something incredibly special was happening, as I knew no man could have this sort of power.

My whole body started to shake, then my legs, which I could hardly lift off the floor at the time, started to jump in the air. I knew something special had happened. As I stood up and walked around the room, there was no longer any pain from the ME and I was walking without my crutches. Barry smiled.

'It appears that Jesus has healed you,' he said.

I sat back in my chair somewhat stunned.

I thanked the Lord in a silent prayer for healing my ME. It had been nineteen years since it had first started to devastate my life. Then I thought back to the prison ward. In the past months I knew God had used me to help others there who were desperate. I flopped back in my chair and bowed my head and prayed a silent prayer. 'Dear Jesus, if I am needed in the ward to help others please do not heal me completely yet, as I will be moved to another part of the prison and will not be able to help. There is one thing though, I cannot get any painkillers for my ME so I would appreciate it if you could tone the pain down a bit. Thank you Lord.'

As I limped back to the ward I remembered what I had asked for. I sure couldn't walk again yet, but all the pain had gone. The amazing thing was that I haven't had any pain from my ME since, yet my joints and muscles were acting the same as usual, like a seized car engine. The encephalitis (brain problems) part of the ME was also to start healing from that day. My mind was returning to normal.

Shortly afterwards Richard felt that God was telling him to pray for healing for a dangerous criminal in the prison hospital.

I remember putting my hands on young Ernie's head and asking the Lord for healing and nothing happened, or did it? The Lord works in his own way and time.

Marshall was sitting up holding his head, joyously shouting that the pain had gone. I staggered back to bed and sat down. I was shaking. My God, I thought, the Lord has used me as a channel and healed someone!

Richard left prison in 1994.

As I came out of the gates of the prison in a wheelchair God said to me, 'You went out on a limb for me and now I will heal your limbs.' As the day went on I was able to get out of my wheelchair and I started to walk better. By the evening I was totally healed. I threw away my crutches and haven't needed them since.

Richard was later remarried to a lady called Liz, the person who first introduced him to God.

Testimonies of Healing on ME Retreats

In 1999 we had a very special retreat week at Lee Abbey in Devon. As a result of that week, not only was an ME sufferer healed, but the vision for the charity of which I am now Patron, Hope for ME, was born. (See Appendix 3.)

Kate gives her testimony below.

Thursday night, after we had a time of prayer ministry, the Lord gave me a picture of ME lying dead on the floor. It was a grey deformed figure. Where the ME once stood there was now a glowing figure with its hands raised in praise. All around and surrounding this figure were rays, shafts and spirals of glorious colours. The word I received was 'ME is dead, it has lost its hold on you, your spirit is alive and from it flow rivers of life.' In the morning I got up and drew this picture, but it felt silly to share it.

Yesterday (Monday) I had an urge all day to record myself singing (this is something I never ever do!). About 2pm, I gave in and began to worship God whilst I was recording myself. After singing for a little while, I began to sing in tongues, and then realized that the Lord was going to do something. I started to receive an interpretation and the Lord was telling me to 'press in'. I continued and he began to say he wanted to touch me, to bless me and refresh me, but I needed to press in to his presence. Then he said, 'I want to restore your body and restore your strength. I'm going to heal you: receive, receive,

receive.' Finally (at which point I began to cry with the realisation of what he was going to do) the Lord said, 'I have healed you, my child.' I couldn't take in what had happened. I rewound the tape and began to listen, at which point the presence of God came all over me and cocooned me. I looked down at my hands and I felt what I can only describe as new life enter my body. I began to cry deeply and my whole body shook. It was a cry of amazement, of awe. I got up still surrounded by his presence and started to shout 'New life! New life! New life!' I ran and danced from room to room, still shouting 'New life!' My body became lighter and fresher. Everything looked and felt different. I spent the rest of yesterday dancing and jumping and running. The weight of ME has left my body and the fog has cleared away! I feel so free. The Lord has restored my health. Glory!!

In 2001, on an ME Caring Break at Carberry Conference Centre near Edinburgh, two long-term severe ME sufferers were healed. One discarded her walking frame and walked unaided for the first time in years, while another literally got up out of her wheelchair and walked! It was like seeing pages from the Bible come to life, witnessing such dramatic healing in response to prayer. Catherine gives her testimony below.

When I went to Carberry on a caring break for those with ME, I had not gone with very high motives. I wanted to meet people whom I had previously only corresponded with.

One afternoon, though, we went into the chapel for a time of prayer ministry. Two members of the team, one recovering from ME and another who had been healed, prayed for me. One of the team asked me what I wanted God to do for me. My ME brain couldn't cope with a question like that. For just over a year I had been struggling with the challenge of healing. I knew God could heal. I just wasn't sure I wanted it! I think I was frightened to ask for healing in case it didn't happen.

In the evening we were given the opportunity to return to the chapel and I met my friend there, with whom I had been in contact for the last five years. She told me how she had walked to the chapel. My jaw must have dropped to the floor! I was amazed that she had got to Carberry at all because of her health. She had arrived before the week started, to get over the journey, but even so, found walking to the main building with her rollator or walking sticks very tiring. Now she said she had walked to the chapel unaided, it was mind-blowing!

The next morning I woke early to hear the Lord say, 'Get out of bed, kneel down and pray.' I answered, 'But Lord, you know that I can't kneel.' Again came the words, 'Get out of bed, kneel down and pray.' The Lord does not often speak to me like this, but tremendous blessings have come in the past when I have obeyed the words I have heard. Although I had not been able to kneel for six years, when my knees hit the floor, my brain cleared, and I could really praise God. It was amazing. God had worked a miracle of healing in my life! Then came the instruction, 'Walk over to the dining room.' In came the doubt. I wasn't sure that I could walk across the grounds, all by myself. But I left the wheelchair behind, and set off, very gingerly, like walking on ice. As I walked I watched the squirrels scampering around and eventually arrived at the empty dining room. What an anti-climax!

Eventually a lady walked in and as I told her that I had walked to the dining room, I burst into tears as the enormity of what had happened hit me. I then found I was able to walk the length of the dining room to get the cereals I wanted. I could even lift a jug of milk by myself, and pour my own tea – yes, the proper stuff with caffeine in it! As people came into the room, they were told of my healing. Someone later asked if I was worried about making the return journey. My answer was 'No', I wasn't sure if I could even get there in the first place!

12

OPEN TO GOD

Surrendering

Being willing to be open to God raises many questions: Is God trustworthy? Can he really help me? What might happen? It is hard for us to surrender ourselves to God, because we like to be in control. However, surrendering to God can be a liberating experience:

> It is like opening the lid of a jar and letting the butterfly wing away freely, or like a person paralysed for years being able to run and jump and dance again. It is the freedom of the bound Lazarus coming forth from the tomb.[1]

Many sufferers, out of sheer desperation, have let go of that control and God has run to meet them. One sufferer, who did not believe in God, was persuaded by some Christian sufferers to go to a healing service. She says, 'They had told me how they had experienced healing through prayer, and I was so desperate that I was totally open to trying anything, even God.' Mary experienced considerable healing that night and is now much better.

As a result of a meditation on creation, one sufferer wrote: 'When I was meditating on some opened and closed daisies, I felt that God showed me that I have to open myself up to him. I have to become vulnerable, like an open flower, in order to be fully exposed to the healing rays of God's glory and grace.'

The following poem by another sufferer speaks of this:

MY ROSE

My child you are like a rose,
A rose not yet in bloom,
A rose in tight, tight bud.

Do not strain my child
To unfurl your petals,
Do not strive to be cleansed from darkness.

My child, my rose,
Put your hand in mine,
Put your hand in the hand of your Saviour.

I will lead you, I will guide you,
Trust me my child.
I have brought you here for a purpose.

Be patient my beautiful one,
For your petals will unfurl
In response to my love.

As the fresh morning dew
Of my Love touches you,
As I nourish your roots
When you feed on my Word,
So your petals will unfurl.

I know your beauty my own one,
I see your beauty that is hidden deep inside,
I have plans for you my rose, such plans,
Trust me.

I cherish you my rose,
I hold your delicate leaves in the palm of my hand,
No harm will come to you.

I will deliver you from evil,
I will wash you and cleanse you and make you new,
But in my time my rose, not yours.

Only I, your Creator, know
When to touch you,
When to release you,
Only I my rose and no other.

So trust me my own one,
Lay your head upon my chest
And know my Peace.

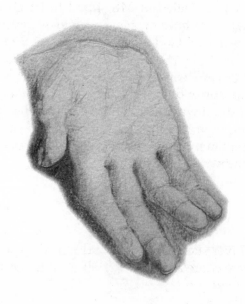

Letting Go

I used to have a sticker on my car, saying 'Let go and let God', which was a reminder to let go of my worries and struggles and give them to God. Little did I realize then that I would have to let go of my beloved Golf GTi too! It was stolen, gutted, vandalized – a write-off. My sticker had been removed and in its place was written 'Happy Easter Ho Ho Ho'. I was due to lead my first ME retreat that Easter and could easily have been unsettled by this violation of my property. However, when I visited the wreckage a few days after the initial identification, the word 'GOD' had somehow appeared, written in large capital letters on the back window. I was astonished. This certainly was not there before. This incident reminded me of the fact that whatever happens to me, God is ultimately in control, and will have the last word!

Before I was healed of ME, I had to let go of all the things that were holding me and release myself totally into the arms of God. I had to take a step into the unknown and place myself completely in his hands. It felt scary, but in a sense I had nothing left to lose. When I let go and surrendered myself totally to God on that particular day, I was already on the road to healing. Over the coming months I began to hear him speaking to me for the first time. He was showing me the way out of ME and the pathway to my healing.

Prayer

Why is prayer such hard work and why does it seem like the ultimate chore at times? Prayer used to remind me of

147

school, only this time God was setting the homework. I knew it was something I had to do, but it was hard to face it and I didn't exactly enjoy it.

Many people wrestle with a lot of guilt over praying and often don't talk about this struggle because they feel they ought to know how to do it. Unfortunately, reading endless books on prayer doesn't particularly help. The much-quoted maxim 'pray as you can, not as you can't' is helpful because it sets us free to discover our own way of praying, however unorthodox.

Prayer speaks of our intimacy with God. Frequently, though, we tend to pray from our heads rather than our hearts, and this can result in meaningless transactions. I recently attended a day conference on prayer, where we talked in groups about all the blockages to prayer. It was encouraging to hear how others, especially some of the clergy, found prayer a struggle. It is hardly surprising that the disciples asked Jesus to teach them how to pray.

The experience of enforced inactivity that I went through seemed to release me into a deeper revelation of prayer. It was something I stumbled across rather than having done anything 'super-spiritual' to achieve it. I simply continued to hand over to God my weaknesses and inability to pray. Part of my struggle was to know how to reach God without the medium of dance – the language through which I most easily gain intimacy with him. Despite my struggles, God used my prayers. Perhaps the sheer frustration of not being able to pray at times, even though I longed to reach God, was a pure prayer in itself. And those times when I felt desperate and was unable to pray, each tear was received into the heart of God as a pure expression of that longing. Our tears are a precious gift to God.

The key to prayer

As I continue on my own journey into prayer, I find my greatest stumbling block is not knowing the true character of God and how much he loves me. This stops me 'approaching the throne with confidence' and inevitably affects my communication with him. This lack of knowledge, along with low self-esteem, creates a barrier in our relationship.

However, through studying the character of God in the Bible and listing all the ways he has shown his love for me, I have been able to challenge my negative thoughts. I am at last beginning to accept the fact that God is 'for' me rather than 'against' me. This journey of personal discovery has proved to be wonderfully liberating. It is also beginning to revolutionize my prayer life as I now see myself walking tall in the knowledge of who I am in God, rather than picturing myself grovelling before him with my head bowed low.

So often we expect to be spoon-fed and taught everything about God, but I believe he longs for us to search for the truth for ourselves, so that our identity is firmly rooted in him. If God loves me just as I am, without me doing anything for him, it releases me from the need to strive to be accepted. God loves me, and so even if I only manage to spend one minute talking to him today, he's delighted. Since I have experienced this liberty, free from condemnation, my prayer life has been more of an adventure than a chore.

The power of prayer

Few of us realize the power we unleash when we ask God to help. Who would have believed that the system of apartheid would collapse in South Africa and that Nelson

Mandela would be set free? It must have seemed like an impossible dream to those who prayed long and hard for there to be a breakthrough. Prayer is dynamic and exciting. It may seem like dialling an empty switchboard at times, but God promises to answer our prayers and rewards our persistence.

When I injured my back in my early twenties and was off work, my friend and her husband offered to pray for me. My reaction was, 'Please yourself.' In a sense, I was humouring them. However, as they prayed and laid hands on me, I felt this incredible heat in my body, and my back began to uncurl. I was able to stand straight for the first time in two weeks. I was utterly amazed, and could hardly believe it. I never forgot this incident; in fact, many years later when I first started to realize that God was telling me that he was going to heal me of ME, I had absolutely no doubt that he could do it, because I'd already experienced his healing power. God had worked miraculously that day, despite my 'please yourself' attitude and indifference to him.

Dr Anne Macintyre writes:

I personally believe that regular prayer by a number of people does bring about healing in the sick person prayed for, even if the recipient does not profess any religious faith. Healing by prayer or by touch cannot be measured scientifically. This is a good thing; we need to believe in miracles in our mechanized, material world. We also need to accept that there are many mysteries in life. Wisdom comes with acceptance of, and belief in, mystery and miracles as well as scientific facts.[2]

Listening to God

I would define prayer as heart-to-heart communication with God, but this is a two-way process. The beauty of silence is that it gives God a chance to get a word in edgeways. Silence may be uncomfortable at first, but creating the time and the space to listen to God has revolutionized my relationship with him. It has made my life easier, not harder, because I have been able to discern God's leading in my life more readily. I know that many struggle to hear that 'still small voice' within, but often it is a question of unscrambling the radio and finely adjusting the tuning until you find God's frequency. Certainly considerable patience is required, but these communications are so precious that it is worth persevering.

God longs to talk to us; in fact, he is thinking about us constantly:

> How precious it is, Lord, to realize that you are thinking about me constantly! I can't even count how many times a day your thoughts turn towards me. And when I wake in the morning, you are still thinking about me!
>
> (Ps. 139:17–18, LB)

And in the Old Testament the prophet Isaiah says, 'You will hear a voice say, "This is the way; turn around and walk here"' (Is. 30:21, NLT).

God can speak to us in a variety of different ways: through the Bible, through dreams and visions, through other people, through creation and creativity, through music, dance and art etc. One sufferer who felt suicidal parked his car on the edge of a cliff. He thought how easy

151

it would be just to release the handbrake. However, when he switched on his car radio the words 'hold on' from REM's song 'Everybody Hurts' arrested him in his tracks. It was as though God were speaking to him directly, saying, 'Hold on, don't do it.'

My Testimony of Healing

Just before the Christmas of 1990, my illness had begun to reach a crisis point. I had to return home to live with my parents, as I was no longer able to look after myself. No matter what treatment I tried, my health deteriorated. There seemed to be no prospect of my returning to teaching or resuming any kind of normal life in the near future. I remember thinking at the time that I could not see the point in living if this were to be my existence. I felt utterly broken. I had come to the end of myself and had no resources left. It was then, in complete desperation, that I surrendered myself totally to God, and from that position of absolute weakness I asked him to heal me. It was like falling backwards. It seemed a tremendous risk, but I had to believe that God would catch me, and he did. As I handed myself completely over to him, he was able to transform my situation.

A few months earlier I had attended a respite week in Dorset for ME sufferers. During that week I became aware that various forms of meditation were becoming popular among ME sufferers, and that is when I began to read *Open to God*[3]. In her book, Joyce Huggett addresses some of the 'barriers and blocks' to a deeper prayer life, offering practical guidance on how to be open to God. The book contains a series of meditations to help the individual 'unearth for themselves the treasures which are buried in the Bible and hidden in their own hearts'.

As I began to read this book, I felt that God was saying to me that Joyce had the answer to my ME. As I had never 'heard' from God before, I thought that this must be wishful thinking. At that time, Joyce and her husband David were leaders at my church, though I didn't really know either of them.

Shortly after that dreadful Christmas in 1990 and the prospect of an even worse New Year, I felt that God was prompting me to attend a parish weekend. This seemed ridiculous to me, as I felt too ill and would probably have to spend most of the time in bed. However, I knew that I was meant to go. Gradually, pieces of God's immense jigsaw began to fit together. During the first session on prayer led by David and Joyce we were encouraged to 'tune in' to what God was saying to each of us. It was rather like finding the right frequency of a particular station on the radio. Before this session, everything seemed so scrambled that I couldn't hear God, nor did I even know on what frequency to look for him. But suddenly it became very clear. The communication lines between myself and God were open. Was I going mad? Did people really hear voices? I could clearly hear God saying that I had suffered long enough, that he wanted to heal me and that I should approach Joyce for prayer. I was reluctant to do this because I felt embarrassed and would have to overcome a considerable amount of pride to ask for help in this way. Consequently, I tried to ignore the message, although it was very persistent. On Sunday, during the final session, God repeated this message with even greater clarity and volume, adding that I would then be free to go and tell others about him. It was now impossible to ignore this message, so I submitted.

As Joyce and another member of the church prayed and laid hands on me, I could feel the power of God's healing love sweeping right through my body. It felt as if plugs had been removed from my feet and all the 'bad' ME blood was draining out of me, being purified and transfused. And in flowed the golden liquid presence of God's love. It was awesome. I had personally experienced God and now knew beyond doubt that he existed. As Joyce held me with my head cradled against her chest, I could identify with the Christ-child secure in Mary's arms, bound by the love of God. It was the first time that I had really experienced God's love and I felt totally secure in his arms.

Shortly afterwards, I went to lie down in my room. I was moved to heartfelt tears that God should want to heal me; that I was worthy of experiencing such depths of God's love and power; and I began to remember the words of the song 'Such Love'.

Not only was I instantly better, but my faith had come alive. Shortly afterwards I wrote:

I can now see God's plan for me. I had to be broken down through ME in order to finally accept him as my personal Saviour. This was the only way I would listen. God did not inflict this illness on me, but allowed it to happen because he had something very special and deep to share with me. I was then malleable, like the potter's clay, and could begin to be moulded in his image. My illness was therefore not 'God's ultimate punishment', as I had sometimes referred to it, but the ultimate learning experience where he would take me on a journey so that I could experience the full reality of him.

My life seems so much richer now, and I gain great pleasure from the simple things in life, which before my illness I had taken for granted. I have been set free from my goldfish bowl existence, I am no longer an envious spectator but a full participant able to venture into the world outside again.

Sampling freedom

Shortly after I was healed I wrote:

> I cannot begin to put into words the sheer joy I experienced as a result of my new-found freedom. I had the energy to be excited by life again. My friends and colleagues were delighted to hear my news, and many could even see the difference in me before I declared, 'I'm healed'. It was wonderful watching the expressions on their faces, and some were moved to tears. My friends noticed a new radiance in me. My old spark was back and there was now a new energy in my voice. I simply could not stop smiling.

As an ME sufferer, locked into an illness of indefinite length, it is hard to imagine what it is like to be released from prison. In many ways I felt as though I could identify with the story of Job. He passed through a protracted period of intense personal suffering and yet 'the LORD made him prosperous again and gave him twice as much as he had before' (Job 42:10). So much had been stripped away from me, but once I was healed, all my senses seemed to be heightened and it felt as though I could see clearly for the first time. I gazed through the window and observed the glorious winter sunshine dancing on the flowers and trees, knowing that I had the freedom to explore God's magnificent creation. How could I have taken all this for granted before?

Indulging in my first cup of coffee again with all its forbidden chemicals was a real treat, as for many months I had been on a very restricted detoxification programme. Dunking and sampling my first chocolate biscuit caused my taste buds to reel. It was wonderful. The freedom of being able to pop out and see my friends when I wanted to, or invite them round, thrilled me. It really felt such a privilege to be back in the human race again. Even cleaning was an exhilarating experience. For the first time in two years I was able to clean my house thoroughly and no longer needed to worry about being ill afterwards. Now I had freedom and control over my body, I no longer needed to 'pay the price' for everything I did. As I ran out of milk and walked to my local shops for a pint, it struck me that I had not walked along my road for months. I felt like shouting to the neighbours, 'Look, I'm well now. I can even walk to the shops!' The next pleasure I sampled was a trip to Asda. I had the freedom to walk down all the aisles and to choose whatever food I wanted. I felt like a child let loose in a sweet shop, and could almost smell the wonderful aroma of chocolate as I walked past the shelves. Inadvertently, I found myself loading the trolley with at least five different types of thickly coated chocolate biscuits. I had been on 'ration-type' food for long enough. It was time to be decadent. So in went a large bar of Galaxy milk chocolate as well!

After the fiasco of my 30th birthday, when I also fell and broke my arm, my 31st birthday would be very special indeed. This birthday God had given the best birthday present I could ever have hoped for, my freedom.

During the second week in February it snowed heavily. Many people were frustrated by the inconvenience and were feeling incarcerated. I felt both exhilarated and liberated by it. The immense joy of being out in the open air, of seeing God's beauty and magnificence in the white carpeted landscape and experiencing the crisp white snow as it crunched under my feet. I was free. The chains of my illness had fallen off. As the snow was forecast to continue, I hired some ski equipment. My ME had resulted from a viral infection which I had picked up whilst skiing in Andorra and so it was indescribably wonderful to be experiencing the joys of this sport again. My life seemed to have come full circle.

And I pray that you, being rooted and established in love, may have power, together with all the saints, to grasp how wide and long and high and deep is the love of Christ.

(Eph. 3:17–18)

13

EXPLORING CREATIVITY

Behind the Veil

When I was studying for my Masters degree, we learned how the brain is composed of two hemispheres, the left and right, which perform different functions. In our western culture most of us have brains that are more highly developed on the left side than on the right. In other words, we major almost exclusively on left-brain functions, which include reading, writing, talking, reasoning, logic, analysis, competing, achieving, controlling, mastering etc. This is the 'doing' side of the brain. The right-brain functions, which include creativity, musical appreciation, imagery, symbolism, fantasy, experiencing, perceptual, emotions, relaxing, meditation and prayer, tend to be neglected. This is the 'being' side of the brain. A balance between these two sides of the brain is essential for health and well-being.

In a sense, having ME is an opportunity to develop the right side of the brain, because much of the left-brain functioning is impossible for many ME sufferers. So, buried within what sufferers describe as 'brain fog' are 'hidden treasures' waiting to be explored and unearthed. As one sufferer comments, 'Because ME strips so much away, I have found that a whole new perspective opens up if you can develop a purely creative activity.'

Healing Through Creativity

Many sufferers have received emotional, spiritual and physical healing as a result of unveiling their own 'hidden treasures' and nurturing this creative side in themselves.

One sufferer felt that God was telling her she needed to dance to receive her healing. She spent much of her childhood dancing and loved it, but thought it was madness to try, considering how little energy she had. She writes, 'I later attended a Christian healing seminar and danced my heart out. Two people then prayed for me, and the next thing I knew I was resting on the floor. When I got up I was full of energy and vitality. Since then my energy levels have increased enormously and I am now able to lead keep-fit classes again. A whole new area of ministry has also opened up for me in signing for the deaf as well as developing signed dance.'

Maria, a former professional dancer who has chronic scoliosis of the spine and ME, writes:

Today was a bad day. I finally gave up and turned to bed again, hobbling painfully and desperately upstairs. As I went to put something in the wardrobe I caught sight of a reflection in the mirror, and without moving I did a double take. What I saw reflected there was a dancer...well it was me, of course, but I looked like a dancer! My whole body and posture was that of a dancer. As I recognized the dancer that I once was through that reflection, it was as though God was saying that is what I am, from the beginning and for eternity. My disability and deformity cannot undo that which God ordained for me before I was born.

I have always known in my spirit that I shall dance before the Lord in glory, and he has blessed me by being able to dance in the spirit and also in my mind. The full import and paradox of this revelation simply cannot be put into words, but what Paul says in Corinthians explains something which I cannot: 'But God chose the foolish things of the world to shame the wise; God chose the weak things of the world to shame the strong. He chose the lowly things of this world and the despised things – and the things that are not – to nullify the things that are, so that no one may boast before him' (1 Cor. 1:27–30). God's grace is transforming, revealing, redeeming. God has made me a dancer for eternity!

The Treasures in Darkness

And I will give you treasures hidden in the darkness –
secret riches. I will do this so you may know that I am the
LORD, the God of Israel, the one who calls you by name.

(Is. 45:3, NLT)

God has so many facets to his creativity and wants to express that abundance through us, his created beings. Creation is one of the greatest expressions of God's love for us. We are made in the image of the Creator, and it is natural for us to be creative because we are 'a chip off the old block'. Being creative is a powerful form of communication and can bring us into the presence of God.

We are often put off creativity by bad experiences in the past, or we may simply feel that we are not good enough. I believe that anything we create is valuable to God, because it is an expression of who we are and that is precious to him. Just as a parent readily enthuses over and enjoys their child's painting, so God delights in all that we create.

Creativity is an important component of an ME retreat. Many sufferers have experienced considerable healing as a result of developing their creative side. Others have gained valuable insights through art and colour, clay work, poetry, singing and even dancing.

I was very moved when I spoke to one sufferer's 11-year-old daughter, called Lucy. She has accepted the limitations her mother's illness places on her life, but has always wanted to dance. It was a great privilege to spend some time with her on retreat, encouraging her in movement and teaching her how to dance using flags and a gymnastic ribbon. A new joy and freedom seemed to be released in her as both she and her mum, a severe sufferer, expressed themselves through movement.

ME does not have to rob you of everything. It can be an opportunity for new interests and hobbies to emerge. When I became ill, I found it very hard to adjust to not 'doing', because all my hobbies were very active ones. I had always considered more sedentary hobbies boring. ME presented me with a huge challenge, and I began to regret that I had not cultivated other interests. Since then I have discovered that life is an ongoing creative process; that every part of life is creative in some way. Exploring my creativity is now an intimate part of my relationship with God as well as essential for my health.

Jenny writes:

At first writing helped me get through the anger, fear and pain. By writing it down I was facing it and found that, like the Psalmist, once the crying was out of the way I could see a way forward – not always an answer (or not one I necessarily wanted), but a response, as from a parent comforting a fretful child. The breakthrough was and is for me learning to be honest with myself and with God. He gave me, and I gave myself, permission to express my fear, anger, confusion, etc in words. Like the coloured threads of an embroidered picture, there have to be dark threads to give shape and form amongst the light and colour. All is valid. Even pain and anguish – especially pain and anguish. Language is a beautiful way of weaving the expressible, of taking the ordinary coloured threads of our life experiences as emotions and creating an extraordinary picture.

Barbara writes:

When I was able to do very little else I remember making Valentine cards for my two children – it meant a lot to me to tell them I loved them even if I was not able to do much practically for them.

I feel that ME sometimes robs me of expressing who I really am – sometimes it's just too tiring to sit and talk to someone at length. However, expressing oneself in painting or poetry is a very personal expression of who I am. I use painting as a way of expressing how I feel. It helps me to get in touch with my own feelings. For example, I may seem rather lifeless, but I have just painted a picture full of great power and energy with the sea crashing against some rocks on a stormy day. Even if it is only for my own benefit, I feel good that I have expressed something of the real me.

I asked one sufferer who is also an ordained minister how he came to take up clowning. He writes:

Clowning took me up! There's always been a clown in me expressed in a variety of ways. When I discovered that I could 'minister' as a clown, it was a revelation from God. I have learned so much from my clown character GOF (God's own fool). GOF has taught me about the balance between vulnerability and encouragement. The vulnerability of a clown can draw out another person's vulnerability or encouragement and vice versa.

Singing for joy on their beds

On one retreat we were delighted to read in Psalm 149 verse 5 the encouragement that the saints 'sing for joy on their beds'. This meant a lot to one sufferer who had once been a trained singer, but whose gifting had been strangled by ME. Some months later, however, she was asked to sing as soprano soloist at her local cathedral. Two days before the concert she had been taken to the local casualty department because she felt so ill!

However, the day of the concert dawned and I forewarned the conductor that I was ill and unlikely to make it. I felt unwell until 4pm and missed the rehearsal in the afternoon with the orchestra. The conductor had great faith in me, as he had not made alternative arrangements! I had to put my trust in God and felt that if I was meant to be there he would get me there. Sure enough, about 4.30pm the weight of oppression and pain lifted and I began to recover, albeit slowly. I missed the first half of the concert that didn't involve me and I sang in the second half.

A lot of friends were praying for me, and those who came said that they wouldn't have known that anything was wrong! Little did they know that several times the floor came up to greet me, as my balance was anything but normal. Once again God had proved his strength – I am sure he wanted me to sing his praises.

I met Kate, a singer songwriter, on an ME retreat. She was an inspiration. When she sang one of her original songs on the first night, we were all overwhelmed and deeply moved. What talent, what creativity poured out through the wonderfully free and exciting medium of jazz. Kate's greatest joy is to 'communicate something which people in pain can relate to'. Here are the words to her song 'Make Me Whole, Lord':

MAKE ME WHOLE, LORD

Right down deep inside me I have a well of pain
The only thing that brings release, and helps me to feel sane
Is coming to you, Father, and pouring out my heart

Letting you into the pain, into the hurting part …
Make me whole, Lord
Fill this hole, Lord
Please bring healing to the pain I feel.
Choose your will, Lord
As I yield this part of me into your loving hands.

Please give me a vision of how things can be …
Set my eyes on things above, on things I cannot see …
Though I'm feeling weak and frail, fill me with your Spirit

Help me praise the One who raised
My spirit from the grave …

Make me whole, Lord
Fill this hole, Lord
Please bring healing to the pain I feel.
Choose your will, Lord
As I yield this part of me into your loving hands.

(Kate Biernan)

'Like clay in the hand of the potter, so are you in my hand …' (Jer. 18:6)

In the beginning God shaped and formed us in our mother's womb and carved our names on the palms of his hands (Ps. 139:13; Is. 49:16). God continually shapes us and moulds us into the person he created us to be, but we have to be willing to allow him to knead and form us in his image. Being malleable is a vulnerable state to be in, as we surrender ourselves to God and trust in the hands of the Potter.

So I went down to the potter's house, and I saw him working at the wheel. But the pot he was shaping from the clay was marred in his hands; so the potter formed it into another pot, shaping it as seemed best to him (Jer. 18:3–4).

On each retreat, I tend to ask sufferers what their expectations are. One sufferer, Rachel, wrote, 'Mine were seemingly clear-cut – I thought I knew what it would be like, how I'd react and definitely what I would feel. Now, at the end of the retreat, the clay work seems particularly symbolic – representing a remoulding of beliefs, thoughts and actions, unleashing a new way of being.' She expressed her feelings through this poem:

MOULDING CLAY

A lump of clay –
a blank slate,
empty, lifeless and
without form.
Product of the earth
given to mould
and awaiting new life.
With each movement,
each human touch –
turning it,
rolling it,
pressing it –
new formations emerge.

Gradually building
secure and recognisable forms.
Vitality and energy flow
from within,
life engages with clay –
two worlds merge.

Remoulding and reshaping
renewal of thoughts,
reflecting.
The blank slate awakens
takes a new role.

Inner void becomes
inner peace.

(Rachel Newcombe)

Tears that dance

A friend said to me, 'Liz, you may not be able to dance at the moment, but you still have the spirit of a dancer.' I found this a curious statement, but as I thought about it I realized the truth in this. My spirit didn't have to be chained by my current disability; in fact, it could still dance! I began to realize that this is what another friend, a former professional dancer, had meant some years earlier when, despite being in a wheelchair, she spoke of the amazing freedom she experienced when she pictured herself dancing in the spirit. It was a freedom that soared way beyond anything that her body was once capable of.

As a dancer, I have found my greatest challenge has been to develop a dance based on my testimony of healing. It needed to portray very clearly what it was like to suffer with ME, as well as show the release that is possible through God. I collaborated with my friend Deni, who is a sufferer, and asked if she could write a poem specifically for the dance. Even in the writing of that poem Deni received considerable healing.

Using a grey lycra bag to act as a second skin, I was able to convey the torturously slow movements and communicate what it is like to feel trapped inside your own body. Sufferers have been amazed by the dance and encouraged that I have managed to express in movement what they struggle to articulate. The dance is not only a powerful intercession for sufferers, but also a wonderful tool for healing and outreach. Sometimes, when I speak to groups about ME, they forget what I have said, but they never forget the dance! I have even performed the dance on the streets during ME awareness week. Key moments from this dance have now been photographed and published in various magazines and newspapers to help raise awareness of ME.

Morning …
shades of night retreat
and light *hurts*.
Awareness only of another day begun –
the lonely fight continues.
Being alive hurts.
Veins full of lead
hold me down fast to the bed
while dizziness in my head
sends innards spinning.
I feel *sick*.
How long now
have I been awake?
Each movement
effort-filled with ache
and sheer determination …
and so I take
one hour – two, or three
to rise and face
my human habitation.

Afternoon . . . time of trial:
head can make no sense nor rhyme
of conversations, dreams
or time; and space
is taken up by inner fears.
Lots of tears, unshed, unbidden, unseen.
This is
not a dream . . .
but some ungainly being that is me
struggling for its own identity
that has become
a vague and painful memory.

Evening . . .
dread the coming night
with all the failures
of the day in sight –
But this reality stays:
a limping life, a crawling
creature slug-like through
endless days imprisoned in
life turned grey.

LORD ... HEAL ME

14

REACHING OUT TO OTHERS

Talking to People About ME

I believe it is important for sufferers to talk to others about their illness and explain how it is affecting them. I know this is impossible at times because of the concentration and energy required; however, it is only as sufferers open up about the reality of ME rather than hiding behind the 'I'm fine, thanks' comment that people will begin to understand this illness and take it seriously.

The ME dance which I mentioned in the previous chapter is a highly visual portrayal of what it is like to have ME. It has proved to be a good talking point for those unfamiliar with the illness. People have come up to me afterwards, sometimes in a state of shock, and said, 'I had no idea ME was like that.' The dance had clearly made an impact on them. Several people have approached me and apologized for their attitude to sufferers. When I performed the dance in a church setting, some people felt they needed to repent for their condemning and judgemental attitudes to sufferers. Now that is progress!

In 1996 I attended a Christian dance conference where I led a forum on ME. It was surprising how many at that conference either had ME or knew someone with the illness. Even the main speaker, a vicar, had ME. It was a wonderful opportunity to talk about the illness and the vision I believed God was giving me for sufferers. As a result, I met a lady called Pat who has a daughter who suffered with ME. She told me how powerful she found the ME dance and how it reminded her of Lazarus being raised from the dead and coming forth from the tomb. I shared my vision with her and explained how I longed to be able to take sufferers on retreat so that they could 'stand back' from their illness and so find a way forward. Her reply was, 'I think I can help you with that.' Within days, Pat had booked a weekend at Buckfast Abbey and, armed with thirty-five copies of my dissertation on ME, returned to Devon. Four months later I led my first ME retreat, fully backed by her ministry team and forty-plus intercessors praying for the weekend. As I reflected on the message of that dance weekend, the parable of the five loaves and two fishes, I could see that God is able to multiply my little and turn it into much.

The Importance of Reaching Out to Others

Pain and suffering can make us turn in on ourselves, so that we feel like withdrawing from people. This is an understandable but unhealthy reaction and inevitably increases feelings of isolation. I went through a period when I was in so much pain with my knee that I just wanted to withdraw from people. I felt physically and emotionally exposed and vulnerable. I was self-conscious and had lost my confidence to be in a group of people, so I stopped attending several church groups. Even going to church represented a threat to me. I didn't want people to see me hobbling with a walking stick and was embarrassed at communion because I had to stand while everyone else knelt. However, this withdrawal cut

171

me off still further from any source of help both practically and spiritually. My injury already seemed like a form of prison to me at times, but I had further imprisoned myself. It took a tremendous act of the will to break free, but once I'd reached out for help, God blessed me in the most wonderful ways.

There are many scriptures which emphasize the importance of reaching out to other people as well as the benefits and blessings of this.

> Feed the hungry and help those in trouble. Then your light will shine out from the darkness, and the darkness around you will be as bright as day. The LORD will guide you continually, watering your life when you are dry and keeping you healthy, too. You will be like a well-watered garden, like an ever-flowing spring.
>
> (Is. 58:10–11, NLT)

A member of my church reached out to me by inviting me for lunch. As we chatted, she told me how she had been struggling with post-viral fatigue syndrome for the last eighteen months. I asked her if she would mind if I prayed with her. It was good to be able to pray for her, because she had helped me so much in the past. Three weeks later, when I was probably feeling at my lowest, she bounded up to me in church, saying, 'Liz, you know you prayed for me: well the pain has gone and my energy is back. It's wonderful.' I was utterly shocked. What was God doing? I simply didn't understand. Then I remembered the scripture, 'My grace is sufficient for you, for my power is made perfect in weakness' (2 Cor. 12:9).

Theresa, a severe sufferer, who has attended many of the ME retreats, has set up a prayer group. She writes:

The prayer group is very special to me because I am isolated as far as church and Christian ministry is concerned and it is a chance to meet fellow Christians and sufferers in a positive, life-affirming way. So often support groups just talk about the 'awfulness' of the illness. This doesn't happen at the prayer group, because the emphasis is different.

There is hope, we are not abandoned, and God is working out his purposes in our lives. We help to build each other up, comfort one another, pray with one another, and share at a deep level. I think ME is a great leveller and there is an automatic affinity between people who share this incomprehensible, obscure disease. It has been rewarding to see the prayer group grow, with new people hearing about us. I now even send out a newsletter.

Theresa also wrote a letter to encourage me: 'Liz, I know we all look forward to going on the retreats that you lead for us. I think what you are doing is great. You've been healed and are reaching out to minister to others with ME because you know first-hand what ME does to a person. That makes your healing a very powerful statement of faith in action. I hope the book is going well and your knee *will* get better.'

One sufferer told me how her illness meant that she was more available for people and had the time, though not always the energy, to listen: 'People see that I am ill and that I am vulnerable. They are then able to relate to me directly as a human being, rather than seeing me in a role as the vicar's wife.'

I was very moved by the following poem written by Deni:

SHARING

I cannot be with you
in your pain
and I know you cannot share
all of what you are suffering,
but I want you to know that I care.
And if, by knowing,
some part of your journey
is eased,
then take what I can offer you.
And if, by sharing,
some part of your burden
is lifted,
then let me take what you offer me.
And if, by praying,
some part of your pain
finds peace,
then let us pray together.
And if fears and frustrations
anxieties and despair
seem to linger too long to bear,
remember the fact of who you are –
and all that you are a part of –
and let your soul rejoice
in the truth of being
in your Father's love and care.

(Deni Newman)

Allowing Others to Reach In to Us

Sally wrote to me:

> Thank you so much for your note and scripture for me – it arrived this morning and the timing couldn't have been better. I'm really struggling at the moment and am confined to bed with the worst headache I have ever known. I've had it for two weeks so far and live from one lot of painkillers to the next. Your message for me, therefore, was a real boost.
>
> I am praying for your knee and complete healing – it's hard, isn't it, not being able to do the things you love doing. I feel sure the Lord is trying to teach me patience with a capital P (although I sometimes think it's endurance with a capital E!), and I'm not a willing student.
>
> I have been very blessed recently with a lot of care from members of my church. I suppose pride is my main failing in that I hate to be seen to be weak and won't ask for help. These last two weeks, however, I haven't had much option and friends have been taking the children to school, doing my shopping, taking me to the doctor and bringing me flowers. It's hard to receive their love in this way. It makes me feel very humble, but very much loved, and I really value their support and prayers.

It was a great encouragement to receive Sally's card because I knew she understood how I was feeling and that meant a lot and somehow eased my pain. I wrote back:

I'm so sorry you're in such pain at the moment – and yet God is showing you the abundance of his love through those special touches from others. I sometimes see these touches as footprints in the sand – signs that he is there with us, caring for us every step of the way, in the midst of our pain.

My knee has relapsed badly and I can hardly walk at all at the moment, yet I too have been showered with flowers, gifts and loving touches. I agree, it's hard to let go of pride: I struggle with that too. But when we do, somehow it allows God's love for us to bloom and flourish through others. I feel sure that he blesses them for their willingness to give to us. So in a sense, if we don't let others help us we may be depriving them as well as ourselves of God's special blessing.

Praise be to the God ... the Father of compassion and the God of all comfort, who comforts us in all our troubles, so that we can comfort those in any trouble with the comfort we ourselves have received from God.

(2 Cor. 1:3–4)

15

SO WHERE DO I GO FROM HERE?

On Eagle's Wings

The eagle is the king of birds and has a huge wingspan. But its true beauty and majesty can only be fully appreciated when it is seen in flight, which is an awesome sight. The eagle is fiercely protective of its young and will circle above the nest to ward off any potential intruders. When it is time for her young to learn how to fly, however, she pushes them from the nest – but is there to catch them on the wing should they falter. Similarly, God at times seems to push us from a place of comfort in the nest, so that we too can learn to fly. As a result, our faith deepens and we begin to soar even higher in our knowledge of him. We learn to trust the fact that his protective wings are always there to catch us, even if we fall.

I have found that my discomfort and disappointments have been a starting point for transition, growth and change. As I look back, I see that it is the toughest times that have most profoundly influenced who I am and what I have become. Although I sometimes still argue and wrestle with God, various crises have kick-started my faith into action. I haven't wanted religious doctrine; I have just wanted to know whether God could help me, so I've asked him! Every time that I have cried out to God in utter desperation, he has never let me down, and our relationship has soared in renewed intimacy.

The symbol of the eagle speaks of the freedom, strength and release from captivity that is possible in God. In the book of Exodus, God reminds Moses that he so treasures and cherishes his people that he brought them back from captivity in Egypt.

You yourselves have seen what I did to Egypt, and how I carried you on eagles' wings and brought you to myself.

(Ex. 19:4)

Furthermore, he promises to lead his people out of the desert and into the Promised Land, where they will no longer have to endure hardship and will be free for ever. One sufferer explained to me the importance of the image of the eagle:

When I first became a Christian in 1995, I bought my Bible and asked the Lord to show me in the Scriptures that he was going to help me. The first verse I read was Isaiah 40 verse 31.

But they that wait upon the LORD shall renew their strength; they shall mount up with wings as eagles; they shall run, and not be weary; and they shall walk, and not faint (KJV).

This verse has kept me going through the most difficult times. I know the Lord wants me to get well, and this verse says that if I wait (stay, remain) in the Lord he will heal me.

A couple of years later, when I heard this verse set to music as part of a meditation on the ME retreat, I felt the Lord was reaffirming his promise to me. He is faithful and he is a rewarder of those who diligently seek him. He is my only hope, my only prayer.

The following passage of Scripture is a particular favourite of mine because it speaks of the intensity of God's love for us, a love that will go to any lengths to protect and shield from harm. In God we can learn how to soar above our problems as we dare to stretch out the full expanse of our wings and ride the air currents with him.

> He shielded him and cared for him;
> he guarded him as the apple of his eye,
> like an eagle that stirs up its nest
> and hovers over its young,
> that spreads its wings to catch them
> and carries them on its pinions.
>
> (Deut. 32:10–11)

When we learn to place our hope and trust in God, we soar into his presence and leave behind all that binds us.

> But for you who revere my name, the sun of righteousness will rise with healing in its wings. And you will go out and leap like calves released from the stall.
>
> (Mal. 4:2)

'I've had enough, Lord'

These are words uttered by Elijah, an Old Testament prophet (1 Kgs. 19:4). He was struggling with physical exhaustion and emotional and spiritual overload, so he prayed that he might die. He felt he was a failure and couldn't see any answer to the circumstances he found himself in. When suffering with acute exhaustion it is very easy to get things out of perspective. In other words, what I feel may not be the truth of the situation. God adopted a very practical approach with Elijah and told him to rest, eat and come into his presence. In so doing, Elijah was able to receive complete refreshment. God had given him the strength and clarity of vision to go on.

I was reassured to read in one of the gospels that when Jesus met the Samaritan woman, he was not only thirsty, but exhausted: 'Jesus, tired from the long walk, sat wearily beside the well' (Jn. 4:6, NLT). I suppose I've tended to regard Jesus as some kind of miracle-working superhero character. But Jesus ate, slept and needed time to draw apart and rest just as much as we do, because he was human and so also had to wrestle with the weaknesses of the human condition. Jesus' ministry was punctuated by activity and withdrawal. He needed to 'be' with his Father so that he would have the resources to help the huge throngs of people who turned to him.

God Is Faithful

'How long?' are words frequently uttered by the psalmists and echoed by many ME sufferers. In Psalm 13, verses 1 and 2, David wrote:

> How long, O LORD? Will you forget me for ever?
> How long will you hide your face from me?
> How long must I wrestle with my thoughts
> and every day have sorrow in my heart?
> How long will my enemy triumph over me?

It is reassuring that at times David doubted God's presence as well as his timing. However, by the end of the psalm, having poured out his feelings, David is able to trust that God will rescue him from his suffering:

But I trust in your unfailing love;
my heart rejoices in your salvation.
I will sing to the LORD,
for he has been good to me (verses 5–6).

It often seems to me that my least productive times in terms of 'doing' are God's most productive times. When I feel that nothing is happening, there is in fact a lot of hidden growth taking place. It reminds me of a bow and arrow. The arrow has to be drawn backwards in order for it to be propelled forwards at high speed to hit the target. Often our spiritual journey can seem like this. I had little knowledge of what God was achieving in and through me during the period when my life seemed to be 'on hold'. However, I knew it would help if I trusted God in the waiting and co-operated with the process until my leg was restored. God rarely wants us to return to where we were before ME or injury, because he wants to take us forward to a new and better place.

Forget the former things;
do not dwell on the past.
See, I am doing a new thing!
Now it springs up; do you not perceive it?
I am making a way in the desert
and streams in the wasteland.

(Is. 43:18–19)

In 1989, a few months after I became ill with ME, I heard the following passage of Scripture read in church:

The desert will sing and shout for joy . . .
Everyone will see the LORD's splendour,
see his greatness and power.

181

Give strength to hands that are tired
and to knees that tremble with weakness.
Tell everyone who is discouraged,
'Be strong and don't be afraid!
God is coming to your rescue,
coming to punish your enemies.'

The blind will be able to see,
and the deaf will hear.
The lame will leap and dance,
and those who cannot speak will shout for joy ...

They will reach Jerusalem with gladness,
singing and shouting for joy.
They will be happy for ever,
for ever free from sorrow and grief.
(Is. 35, GNB, my emphasis)

I became excited by this scripture and wondered if God
was speaking to me through it, as it seemed to describe
my symptoms exactly, including my paralysed vocal
chord ('those who cannot speak'). Although I didn't
realize it at the time, this was God's promise to me.
Eighteen months later God healed me, and it was only
some weeks afterwards that I remembered how I had
written the whole of Isaiah 35 in the front of my Bible and
dated it July 1989.

Shortly after I was healed I was asked if I would consider going to Jerusalem to dance in the first International
Christian Dance Conference. How could I refuse, when
this scripture was literally unfolding before my eyes? So I
went to Jerusalem, singing and dancing for joy! It never
ceases to amaze me how my life then, and even now,
seems to have unfolded through this passage. *God is
faithful to keep his promises.*

'Behold, I Stand at the Door and Knock ...'

One of the most moving works of sacred art that I have
ever seen is Holman Hunt's remarkable painting *The
Light of the World.* I used to wander into St Paul's
Cathedral in London when visiting my father, who was
in hospital receiving experimental cancer treatment.
These visits tended to be quite harrowing, as his life
seemed so often to hang in the balance, yet somehow I

used to draw great comfort from looking at this inspirational work of art.

The picture is based on a verse in the book of Revelation which reads:

> Behold, I stand at the door and knock; if anyone hears and listens to and heeds My voice and opens the door, I will come in to him and will eat with him, and he [will eat] with Me.
>
> (Rev. 3:20, Amp)

In the picture, the doorway is overgrown with weeds and there is no handle visible. Jesus gently knocks at the door, but only the individual inside can decide whether or not to let him in, because the handle of the door is on the inside. This picture symbolizes the choice we have: Do we dare to let Jesus, 'The Light of the World', into our hearts, or do we continue to shut him out? Jesus will not force his way in like some unscrupulous salesman; he will wait to be asked. We can learn much from other people's experience of God, but in the end God says to each of us, 'Come, experience me and find out for yourself.' One sufferer who had been searching for God wrote:

> I had so many questions and such a lot of curiosity. I realized I'd been struggling so much for answers to everything, and that I needed to let go and relax about it. I was making it all so complicated. As someone who likes concrete facts before making a commitment to anything, the decision whether to go further and become a Christian had weighed very heavily on me. The bottom line was that I didn't have to take everything on board at once. I didn't

have to completely reject all I'd believed or accepted overnight. Becoming a Christian wasn't about a personality transplant! But I still had to put my trust in Jesus and accept him.

I realized I did not have a lot to lose. In fact, I had everything to gain. I'm not just talking about physical healing. Whenever I'd been in the presence of people who really believed in the power of Jesus, whenever I'd been with people really praising him, it seemed so simple; God was definitely there. Whenever I got closer to God I felt so much happier and at peace. I came to realize that I needed my own personal relationship with God rather than leaning on other people's faith and prayers.

The passage from Revelation was originally given to the church. But there is a message in here too for those of us who have hardened our hearts towards God. Do we dare to allow God, through his Holy Spirit, to enter every corner of our lives, or are there still parts that we want to conceal and restrict his access to? In a sense, these are the doorways that have become overgrown with weeds. Do we allow God into every area of our life? Or are we wanting to keep some places hidden from him? Are we dependent on something or someone, and unwilling to let go? A famous French ballerina said, 'You know when you are dependent on something, because you can't bear to let go of it.'

God wants to fill all the spaces, because it is only then that we can experience true freedom and wholeness. God, our loving Father, has our best interests at heart. I know that when I have been willing to hand over another area of my life to God, he has more than filled the empty void, and as a result I have experienced a new depth of freedom and joy. Sometimes God will use our illness or injury to remind us of those unsurrendered areas and invite us to do something about them. This process may be painful, but God promises to bind up and heal our deepest wounds.

> You will seek me and find me when you seek me with all your heart. I will be found by you ... and will bring you back from captivity.
>
> (Jer. 29:13–14)

Becoming a Christian is not about a 'personality transplant', nor do we have to worry about 'becoming a clone', as one sufferer commented. God respects our individuality and made each of us unique. If you feel you would like to commit or recommit your life to Jesus Christ, you may like to pray the following prayer:

> Lord Jesus, I acknowledge you in my pain, anger, frustration, fear and uncertainty. I know that you are my refuge and that I can shelter under your mighty wings of protection. Lord, come into the centre of my life now, and forgive me all my sins. Release me into the fullness of life in your presence through Jesus Christ who died for me. Lord, I know you are able to restore me totally, body, soul and spirit, through the power of your Holy Spirit. I thank you that you say that you will 'restore the years the locusts have eaten'. I choose to put my trust in you now, knowing that you have a perfect plan for my life.

If you would like to find out more about the Christian faith in a friendly, non-threatening environment, you may like to try an Alpha Course. (See Appendix 3.)

A prayer for healing

In the Gospel of Matthew two blind men begged Jesus for healing. Jesus said to them, 'Do you believe that I am able to do this?' 'Yes, Lord,' they replied (Mt. 9:28). Imagine Jesus asking you this same question and consider your response before praying the following prayer:

> Lord, bring your healing and wholeness into every part of my body. Lord, I give you my illness and acknowledge that you are greater than ME. Cleanse my whole body from any virus that still lingers there. Transfuse my blood by the power of your Holy Spirit and fill me with your presence. Lord, I surrender all of my being to you and ask that you would cause my body to function in the way you created it to. I thank you that you are a great and mighty God and that nothing is too difficult for you.

> Praise the LORD, I tell myself,
> and never forget the good things he does for me.
> He forgives all my sins
> and heals all my diseases.
> He ransoms me from death
> and surrounds me with love
> and tender mercies.
> He fills my life with good things.
> My youth is renewed like the eagle's!
>
> (Ps. 103:2–5, NLT)

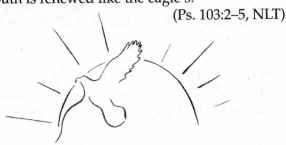

EPILOGUE

BEYOND ME

[God] is able to [carry out His purpose and] do superabundantly, far over and above all that we [dare] ask or think [infinitely beyond our highest prayers, desires, thoughts, hopes, or dreams].

(Eph. 3:20, Amp)

When I originally wrote this book in 1998, I had a serious knee injury and was unsure whether I'd walk again. But the combination of operation, rehabilitation and prayer resulted in my being not only able to walk again but to dance. We take our health and mobility so much for granted, but I have discovered that even the ability to walk is a gift – as I know many ME sufferers would agree.

Since this book was first published in 1999, my life has taken many twists and turns. Being physically healed of ME does not guarantee you a problem-free journey through life. Last year, I suffered with burnout for six months. I think many people assumed that I had developed ME again or had not been healed in the first place. Some even assumed I had ME when I had my knee injury too. Burnout is very different from ME, and I remember only too clearly the cocktail of symptoms I suffered with ME. However, six months of enforced rest and inactivity have been another great lesson. It has made me realize that the achievement-orientated junkie I refer to in the beginning of this book is still alive and kicking. But with God's help and leading, together with

188

my friends' supportive challenges, I *am* negotiating a new path.

Many see busyness as a sign of success in our culture, but I don't. While others were excited about all the opportunities I was having to write books, voice CDs, speak at major conferences, lead retreats, broadcast on radio and TV etc, I was drowning in a sea of overwork and deadlines. I now realize that I don't have to be speeding down the motorway of life to be credible or successful, neither do I need to prove to the sceptics that I am healed of ME. I am discovering that the key to serving God is to spend enough time with him. It's far more important that I am led by God at his speed, rather than driven by my own desires and ambitions. In a sense, that drivenness probably comes from a need to be accepted, but I am increasingly realising that my spiritual home is in God and those precious six months threw me straight back into his arms. God loves me whether I'm busy or not. He loves me whether I write another book or am flat on my back. And he loves you just the same. There's nothing you can do to make him love you more than he does right now.

I'm aware, as I write this, of those sufferers whose lives seem to have stood still, and how hard this must be to cope with. Many must be asking God, 'Why?' The only satisfactory response I've heard to this question was from Joni Eareckson Tada, who said, when asked this, that God rarely answers our 'Whys', because he has given us the gift of himself. As *Can God Help ME?* is republished, my prayer is that all who read it might know 'how wide and long and high and deep is the love of Christ' (Eph. 3:18).

APPENDIX 1

ME RESEARCH INFORMATION

Research Findings

Scientific research into ME/CFS has shown:

1   The presence of enteroviral particles in more than half the muscle biopsies taken from ME patients.

Bowles, N.E., et al., 'Persistence of enterovirus RNA in muscle biopsy samples suggests that some cases of chronic fatigue syndrome result from a previous inflammatory myopathy', *Journal of Medicine* 24 (1993): 145–60.

Gow, J.W., et al., 'Enteroviral sequences detected by polymerase chain reaction in muscle biopsies of patients with post viral fatigue syndrome', *British Medical Journal* 302 (1991): 692–6.

2   Damage to muscle tissue. In one study 80 per cent of the biopsies showed clear evidence of structural damage to mitochondria.

Behan, W.M.H., et al., 'Mitochondrial abnormalities in the post viral fatigue syndrome', *Acta Neuropathologica* 83 (1991): 61–5.

3   Lesions in the brains of approximately 80 per cent of those tested. According to researchers, these lesions are probably caused by inflammation.

Buchwald, D., et al., 'A chronic illness characterized by fatigue, neurologic and immunologic disorders and active human herpes type 6 infection', *Annals of Internal Medicine* 116.2 (1992): 103–13.

Costa, D.C., Tannock, C., and Brostoff, J., 'Brainstem perfusion is impaired in patients with chronic fatigue syndrome', *Quarterly Journal of Medicine* 88 (1995): 767–73.

4   Evidence of an overactive immune system.

Hilgers, A., and Frank, J., 'Chronic fatigue syndrome: evaluation of 30-criteria-score and correlation with immune activation', *Journal of Chronic Fatigue Syndrome* 2.4 (1996): 35–47.

5   A number of disturbances in the function of the hypothalamic-pituitary-adrenal axis.

Bakheit, A.M.O., et al., 'Possible upregulation of hypothalamic 5-hydroxytryptamine receptors in patients with post viral fatigue syndrome', *British Medical Journal* 304 (1992): 1010–12.

Demitrack, M., Dale, J., Straus, S., et al., 'Evidence for impaired activation of the hypothalamic-pituitary-adrenal axis in patients with chronic fatigue syndrome', *Journal of Clinical Endocrinology and Metabolism* 73 (1991): 1224–34.

6   Neuropsychological abnormalities which are consistent with an organic brain disorder.

Rico, M., et al., 'Neuropsychological and psychiatric abnormalities in myalgic encephalomyelitis: a preliminary report', *British Journal of Clinical Psychology* 31 (1992): 111–20.

7   The depression experienced by patients with ME is different from that reported by psychiatric patients and closely related to the severity of other symptoms.

Hickie, I., et al., 'The psychiatric status of patients with chronic fatigue syndrome', *British Journal of Psychiatry* 156 (1990): 534–40.

Shanks, M.F., and Ho-Yen, D.O., 'A clinical study of chronic fatigue syndrome', *British Journal of Psychiatry* 166 (1995): 798–801.

8   The immunological changes documented in ME/PVFS are related to the severity of the illness and correlated with the presence of cognitive dysfunction.

Lutgendorf, S.K., et al., 'Immune functioning predicts cognitive difficulties in chronic fatigue syndromes', *Psychosomatic Medicine* 55 (1993): 100 (Abstract).

9   An association between 'neurally mediated hypotension' and CFS.

Bou-Holaighah, I., Rowe, P.C., Kan, J., and Calkins, H., 'The relationship between neurally mediated hypotension and the chronic fatigue syndrome',

Journal of the American Medical Association 274.12 (1995): 961–7.

(Extensive scientific research details on ME/CFS can be obtained through the ME Association or Action for ME).

Other Useful Research Information and Publications

- I would highly recommend Dr Charles Shepherd's book *Living with ME* (London: Random House 1998) and Dr Anne Macintyre's book, *M.E. Chronic Fatigue Syndrome: A Practical Guide* (London: Thorsons, 1998). Both authors are doctors who suffer with ME.
- I also recommend Doctor David Bell's book *The Doctor's Guide to Chronic Fatigue Syndrome: Understanding, Treating and Living with CFIDS* (US: Perseus Books).

Medical Journals with Web Sites Include:

The British Medical Journal: www.bmj.com
The Lancet: www.thelancet.com
The Journal of the American Medical Association: www.jama.ama-assn.org

Other Useful ME/CFS Sites Include:

- The American Association for Chronic Fatigue Syndrome, which includes an extensive bibliography: www.aacfs.org

- The CFIDS Association (publisher of the CFIDS Chronicle) has an excellent web site with regular research reviews: www.cfids.org
- Cheney Clinic Information Service – information on many forms of treatment available in the US: www.joeant.com
- Chronic Fatigue Support.com – the largest CFS site on the web: www.chronicfatiguesupport.com
- Peer-reviewed medical articles on CFS: www.cfsresearch.org
- US-based site offering research and treatment features on ME, message board service and chat room: www.immunesupport.com
- Information on research and medical theories on topics relating to ME: www.co-cure.org
- Web site of the 25% Group – a nationwide charitable organisation set up to offer support services to those severely affected by ME: www.25megroup.org
- The complete ME tips collection A–Z: www.metips.co.uk
- Email support group for ME patients and families plus web site sharing advice, experiences, reviews and useful links: www.mechat.co.uk
- Christian charity offering friendship and prayer support to all ME sufferers: www.hopeforme.info
- Web site to encourage young Christians with ME: www.godinm-e.co.uk
- Free noticeboard service to help put single people with ME in touch with each other: www.mesingles.org.uk
- Friendship site helping people with ME and their carers find others for mutual support across the UK: www.meconnection.co.uk

APPENDIX 2

ME ORGANIZATIONS

UNITED KINGDOM

Action for ME
PO Box 1302
Wells
BA5 1YE
Telephone: 01749 670799
Web site: www.afme.org.uk
Email: admin@afme.org.uk
Telephone support service: 0117 904 6641 11am–1pm weekdays
A welfare rights helpline and a telephone counselling service are also available for members, together with a list of local support groups.

AYME (The Association of Youth with ME)
PO Box 605
Milton Keynes
MK2 2XD
Telephone: 08451 232389
Web site: www.ayme.org.uk
Email: info@ayme.org.uk
The largest national children's charity for young ME sufferers. Membership free for under-26s.

The ME Association
4 Top Angel
Buckingham Industrial Park
Buckingham
MK18 1TH
Telephone: 01280 816115
Web site: www.meassociation.org.uk
Email: meconnect@meassociation.org.uk
ME Connect provides information and support for sufferers.
Members' Line: 0870 444 1835
Non-members' Line: 0871 222 7824

The National ME Centre
Harold Wood Hospital
Disablement Services Centre
Gubbins Lane
Romford
RM3 0BE
Telephone: 01708 378050
Web site: www.nmec.org.uk
Email: nmecent@aol.com

TYMES Trust (The Young ME Sufferer)
PO Box 4347
Stock
Ingatestone
CM4 9TE
Telephone: 01245 401080
Web site: www.youngactiononline.com

USA

The CFIDS Association of America (chronic fatigue and immune dysfunction syndrome)
PO Box 220398
Charlotte
NC 28222–0398
USA
Telephone: 00 1 704 365 2343
Web site: www.cfids.org

The National CFIDS Foundation
103 Aletha Road
Needham
MA 02492
USA
Telephone: 00 1 781 449 3535
Web site: www.ncf-net.org

APPENDIX 3

OTHER USEFUL INFORMATION AND ADDRESSES

Alpha
Holy Trinity Brompton
Brompton Road
London
SW7 1JA
Telephone: 0845 644 7544
Web site: www.alpha.org.uk
Email: info@alphacourse.org
Alpha is a very popular and highly successful course for those who want to find out more about the Christian faith or brush up on the basics. The course is non-denominational and normally lasts ten weeks, meeting once a week. Alpha courses are available nationally and internationally.

The Association of Christian Counsellors (ACC)
29 Momus Boulevard
Coventry
CV2 5NA
Telephone: 0845 124 9569/9570
Web site: www.acc-uk.org
Email: office@acc-uk.org
The Association will provide information on accredited Christian counsellors in your area.

The British Association for Counselling and Psychotherapy (BACP)
BACP House
35–37 Albert Street
Rugby
CV21 2SG
Telephone: 0870 443 5252
Web site: www.bacp.co.uk
Email: bacp@bacp.co.uk
The Association will provide information on qualified counsellors in your area.

Burrswood Christian Hospital
Groombridge
Tunbridge Wells
TN3 9PY
Telephone: 01892 863637
Web site: www.burrswood.org.uk
Email: admin@burrswood.org.uk
Burrswood offers a blend of medicine, prayer and individual counselling, and aims to treat the whole person body, mind and spirit. The care team includes doctors, nurses, physiotherapists, chaplains and counsellors. Burrswood offers post-operative care, respite and terminal care, as well as care for ME sufferers.

Carers Christian Fellowship
14 Cavie Close
Swindon
SN5 5XD
Telephone: 01793 887068
Web site: www.carerschristianfellowship.org.uk
Email: sjones.ccf@ntlworld.com

Carers UK
20/25 Glasshouse Yard
London
EC1A 4JT
Telephone: 020 7490 8818
Carers' Line: 0808 8087777 Wed and Thur 10am–12pm
and 2pm–4pm
Web site: www.carersonline.org.uk
Email: info@ukcarers.org
Information and support to all carers. Carers' line is a free
telephone advice information service.

Catholic Marriage Centre
Oasis of Peace
Penamser Road
Porthmadog
LL49 9NY
Telephone: 01766 514300
Web site: www.catholicmarriagecentre.org.uk
Email: info@catholicmarriagecentre.org.uk
A Christian residential centre offering retreats for
marriage. Also courses for marriage healing and enrich-
ment, with prayer and counselling.

Cruse
Cruse Bereavement Care
Cruse House
126 Sheen Rd
Richmond
TW9 1UR
Telephone: 020 8939 9530
Helpline: 0870 167 1677
Web site: www.crusebereavementcare.org.uk
Email: helpline@crusebereavementcare.org.uk
Provides help for those who are bereaved. Free
counselling available by trained volunteers.

DIAL (Disablement Information and Advice Lines) UK
St Catherine's
Tickhill Road
Doncaster
DN4 8QN
Telephone: 01302 310123
Web site: www.dialuk.org.uk
Email: enquiries@dialuk.org.uk
Free confidential advice on a variety of issues concerning disabled people.

Disability Benefits Enquiry Line: 0800 882200. Gives advice on sickness and disability benefits as well as carer's benefits.

The GOD Channel
The Angel Foundation
Crown House
Borough Road
Sunderland
SR1 1HW
Telephone: 0870 6070446
Web site: www.god.tv
The GOD Channel broadcasts two Christian television channels that can be received by satellite or cable.

Marriage Care
Clitherow House
1 Blythe Mews
Blythe Road
London
W14 0NW
Telephone: 020 7371 1341
Telephone help line: 0845 660 6000 Mon and Fri 10am–4pm

Web site: www.marriagecare.org.uk
Email: info@marriagecare.org.uk
A Catholic organisation with 63 centres located in and around major towns offering a professional counselling service free of charge, on a non-judgemental basis, to those experiencing difficulties in their close relationships. In addition, the telephone help line provides a first stop, confidential listening and information service.

The MEACH Trust
25 Turnpike Way
Ashington
RH20 3QG
Telephone: 01903 891386
Web site: www.meach.org
Email: info@meach.org
A charity formed to provide specialized residential accommodation and care for patients suffering from severe and chronic ME.

Princess Royal Trust for Carers
Head Office
142 Minories
London
EC3N 1LB
Telephone: 020 7480 7788
Web site: www.carers.org
Email: help@carers.org
Provides information, support and practical help for carers through its growing number of Carers' Centres across the UK.

RADAR (The Royal Association for Disability and
Rehabilitation)
12 City Forum
250 City Road
London
EC1V 8AF
Telephone: 020 7250 3222
Web site: www.radar.org.uk
Email: radar@radar.org.uk
Umbrella organisation giving advice on all matters
related to disability.

Relate
Herbert Gray College
Little Church St
Rugby
CV21 3AP
Telephone: 0845 456 1310
Web site: www.relate.org.uk
Email: enquiries@relate.org.uk
Provides counselling and therapy to couples or
individuals having problems with their relationships.

The Samaritans
Telephone: 08457 909090
Web site: www.samaritans.org.uk
Email: jo@samaritans.org
Provide confidential emotional support to anyone in
crisis, with special concern for those who feel suicidal.

Sozo Ministries International
Sozo House
Alma Road
Romsey
SO51 8ED
Telephone: 01794 522511
Web site: www.sozo.org
Email: email@sozo.org
Some sufferers have been healed of ME through this ministry.

Through the Roof (Disabled Christian Fellowship)
PO Box 353
Epsom
KT18 5WS
Telephone: 01372 749955
Web site: www.throughtheroof.org
Email: info@throughtheroof.org

Tourism for All
7th Floor
Sunley House
4 Bedford Park
Croydon
CR0 2AP
Telephone: 0845 124 9971
Web site: www.tourismforall.org.uk
Email: info@holidaycare.org
Provides information on specialist holidays available to disabled people and their carers.

United Christian Broadcasters (UCB)
PO Box 255
Stoke-on-Trent
ST4 8YY
Telephone: 01782 642000
Web site: www.ucb.co.uk
Email: ucb@ucb.co.uk
The UCB Prayer Line offers help, prayer and information
on the Christian faith. Telephone 0845 456 7729 Mon–Fri
9.30 am–10.30 pm
UCB broadcasts four Christian radio channels and a
Christian TV channel via cable or satellite.
UCB also publishes an excellent booklet of daily Bible
readings called *The Word for Today*, which can be obtained
free from the above address. I have found it to be a great
source of encouragement.

SPECIAL INTEREST GROUPS

25% ME Group
4 Douglas Court
Beach Road
Barassie
Troon
KA10 6SQ
Web site: www.25megroup.org
Email: enquiry@25megroup.org
A group for severely affected ME sufferers.

ACW (The Association of Christian Writers)
The Administrator
All Saints Vicarage
43 All Saints Close
Edmonton
London
N9 9AT
Telephone: 020 8884 4348
Web site: www.christianwriters.org.uk
Email: admin@christianwriters.org.uk

CDFB (The Christian Dance Fellowship of Britain)
Julie Latham
Dell Side House
Station Road
Broadley
Whitworth
OL12 8RT
Telephone: 01706 351951
Web site: www.cdfb.org.uk

ME Prayer Fellowship
Carolyn Jowett
Maranatha
16 Glenrose Drive
Bradford
BD7 2QQ
Telephone: 01274 570954
Email: carolyn@jowett.fsnet.co.uk

RETREATS

Many sufferers contact me about retreats. There are a variety of retreats and breaks that sufferers can attend if they are well enough. Action for ME runs respite weeks near Bath. Carberry Tower, which I mention in Chapter 11, is a Christian Conference Centre and it holds two ME caring breaks a year in April and October. 'Hope for ME', the Christian charity of which I am Patron, runs retreat days in the East Midlands area. Unfortunately, I no longer have time to run my own ME retreats, but am often invited as a guest speaker. To find out about my forthcoming engagements and new publications, consult my web site: www.lizbabbs.com

Carberry Residential Christian Centre
Musselburgh
Midlothian
EH21 8PY
Telephone: 0131 665 3135
Web site: www.carberry.org.uk
Email: office@carberry.org.uk

Hope for ME
Jacquie Taylor
3 The Courtyard
Church Lane
Waltham On The Walds
LE14 4AE
Telephone: 01664 464395
Web site: www.hopeforme.info
Email: jacquietaylor@hopeforme.info
Hope for ME is a small Christian charity that offers friendship and prayer support to all ME sufferers. It is free to join and there is a bi-monthly newsletter.

Alternatively, you could go on retreat to one of the many retreat centres across the UK. Details of a variety of retreats and retreat houses are given in *Retreats* magazine. For details contact:
The Retreat Association
256 Bermondsey Street
London
SE1 3UJ
Telephone: 0845 456 1429
Web site: www.retreats.org.uk
Email: info@retreats.org.uk

RESOURCES OF MINE THAT SUFFERERS MAY FIND HELPFUL

- Many ME sufferers find that they are not well enough to go on retreat, and so I would recommend my relaxation and meditation CD *A Quiet Place*, which includes the material and music that I have used on my ME retreats. *A Quiet Place* CD £13.99 (Stowmarket: Kevin Mayhew 2004). Also available through Kingsgate Publishing in the US.

- If prayer is a problem and you're feeling really low, I'd recommend my book and CD *Out of the Depths*, which has helped many sufferers emerge from the pit of darkness. *Out of the Depths* CD £13.99 (Stowmarket: Kevin Mayhew 2004). *Out of the Depths* colour gift book £5.99 (Stowmarket: Kevin Mayhew 2004). Also available through Kingsgate Publishing in the US.

- *The Celtic Heart* is also helping many sufferers to improve the quality of their relaxation, as well as draw closer to God. *The Celtic Heart* colour gift book and instrumental CD £7.99 (Oxford: Lion Hudson 2003).

- Christian meditation was a pathway to my own healing from ME. My book *Into God's Presence* will help you to discover more about relaxation and meditation, as well as how to hear and be guided by God's voice. *Into God's Presence – Listening to God Through Prayer and Meditation* £8.99 (Grand Rapids, Michigan: Zondervan 2004).

All these publications can be ordered through my web site www.lizbabbs.com or from bookshops both here and in the US. You can also contact me via my web site www.lizbabbs.com

NOTES

Chapter 1

1. C.P. McEvedy and A.W. Beard, 'Royal Free Epidemic of 1955 – a reconsideration', *British Medical Journal*, 1970, 1, 7–11.
2. A. Ramsay, *Postviral Fatigue Syndrome: The Saga of the Royal Free* (London: Gower Medical Publishing, 1986).
3. Dr Anne Macintyre, *ME. How to live with it* (London: Thorsons, 1988). Reprinted by permission of HarperCollins Publishers Ltd. © Dr Anne Macintyre 1988.

Chapter 2

1. Dr Belinda Dawes and Dr Damien Downing, *Why ME?* (London: Grafton Books, 1990) p 5.
2. Richard Guest, *A Loving Father* (Cornwall: Tredenham Publishing, 1995).

Chapter 3

1. Dr Anne Macintyre, *ME. How to live with it* (London: Thorsons, 1988).

Chapter 4

1. Aelred of Rievaulx. Text written on a prayer card I picked up from Mount Saint Bernard Abbey.

Chapter 5

1. Dr Charles Shepherd, 'Your Medical Director – What Does He Do?', *Perspectives* (The magazine of the ME Association), issue 60, p vii. Used by kind permission of the ME Association.
2. Dr Anne Macintyre, *ME. How to live with it* (London: Thorsons, 1988) p xiii. Used by kind permission of the Ramsay family.
3. Dr Anne Macintyre, ibid.
4. Dr Clare Fleming, 'The Glass Cage', *British Medical Journal*, 19 March 1994, vol. 308, p 797.

Chapter 6

1. Kathryn Green, *Kathryn's story* (Lincs.: Autumn House, 1995), p 58–9.
2. Kathryn Green, ibid.

Chapter 7

1. Frankie Campling, 'One kind of bereavement', *Perspectives*, issue 61, p 14. Used by kind permission of the ME Association.
2. Jane Grayshon, *In Times of Pain* (Oxford: Lion 1990), p 24. Used by kind permission of Lion Hudson plc.
3. Frankie Campling, op cit. Used by kind permission of the ME Association.
4. Krysia Przybora, 'In the Tunnel of ME,' *Carer and Counsellor*, vol. 3, no. 1, 1993, p 25.

Chapter 8

1. Dr C. Shepherd and H. Lees, 'ME: Is it a genuine disease?' *Health Visitor*, vol. 65, no.5, p 165. Used by kind permission of the ME Association.
2. Revd Leonard C. Wilson, *Meditation – Why and How?* (East Sussex: The Divine Healing Mission).
3. Eileen and Kathleen Egan. *Blessed are You* (London: Fount 1992), p 102.

Chapter 9

1. Gerard W. Hughes, *God of Surprises* (London: Darton, Longman & Todd, 1992), p 34.
2. From 'Footprints' by Margaret Fishback Powers. Copyright (©) 1964 by Margaret Fishback Powers. Reprinted by permission of HarperCollins Publishers Ltd., Toronto, Canada.

Chapter 10

1. Jennifer Rees Larcombe, *Beyond Healing* (London: Hodder and Stoughton, 1986) and *Unexpected Healing* (1991).

Chapter 11

1. Richard Guest, *A Loving Father* (Cornwall: Tredenham Publishing, 1995).

Chapter 12

1. Joyce Rupp, *Praying Our Goodbyes* (Guildford: Eagle, 1995), p 101.

2. Dr Anne Macintyre, *M.E. Chronic Fatigue Syndrome: A Practical Guide* (London: Thorsons, 1998), p 246–7.
3. Joyce Huggett, *Open to God* (Suffolk: Kevin Mayhew, 2004).

Every effort has been made to trace and acknowledge copyright holders of all the quotations in this book. We apologize for any errors and omissions that remain, and would ask those concerned to contact the publishers, who will ensure that full acknowledgement is made in the future.

ARTISTIC ACKNOWLEDGEMENTS

Chapter 8: Sister Theresa Margaret CHN. Stella Brookes – 'The Prodigal'.

Chapter 9: Sister Theresa Margaret CHN.

Chapter 11: Jacquie Anderson – 'Open Hand'. Stella Brookes – 'Such Love'.

Chapter 12: Stella Brookes – 'The ME Dance'.

Chapter 14: Stella Brookes – 'Liz Dancing in Worship'. Honor Day – 'On Eagle's Wings'.